A.Z.

May you find
inspiration in this
little treasure.

Love Bobby

2015

The journey of the human spirit is a wondrous voyage from a primitive state of ignorance, going through innumerable lifetimes in which one grows in wisdom, until at last one merges with all spirits in a state of absolute love and light. And the journey doesn't stop there but continues on, for then one becomes part of Creation and actively participates as a co-creator of new universes. On and on, say the Pleiadians, one progresses into greater love and light, into more and more glorious adventures. This book is written for those who want a way of life and a perspective that truly enables them to grow spiritually— to find deep inner happiness and a wonderful freedom of spirit. Pleiadian Spirituality is for those willing to take complete responsibility for their own lives, for those who have seen through the false promises of religions, cults, and gurus and yet are still seeking greater spiritual development.

This little book is yet the best introduction to the essence of the Billy Meier contact case, of which continues to this day. Gene Andrade culled information from a variety of sources as he compiled this work, all of which were based on (unofficial) translations from the original German documents done in the 1980's by other researchers such as Lt. Col. Wendelle Stevens.

Since this book was published in 1997, there have been many corrections, updates and clarificatins in the translated English versions of the material/information. Due to the nearly insurmountable callenges in accurately translating from German to English, the correct meanings and many important details were lost.

There is a body of books and literature that is correctly translated to English from the original German that is available to everyone.

25 years ago, I began an intentional journey to find answers to a great many questions. I repeatedly found myself right back here with Eduard Albert Meier (Billy) of Switzerland, and the basic spiritual principles and ideals brought to us, once again from the Stars.

It brings me the greatest joy to share it with you.

Bob Foster

STAR WISDOM
Principles of Pleiadian Spirituality

Gene Andrade

FOSTER/ZAHARIAS
132 Deer Park Road • Port Angeles, WA. 98362

Published by

The Pleiades Project
P. O. Box 1270
Rancho Mirage, CA 92270

Many thanks to Ann West for her
guidance, suggestions, and support.

And thanks to all those who were kind enough to read early
drafts of this book and who offered their suggestions.

Most of all, thanks to Eileen Maceri for her ongoing
encouragement, support, and superb copyediting and
proofreading of draft after draft of this book.

Cover art by David Dees
Inside illustrations by Beth Garcia

ISBN 1-885-757-10-7

Printed in the USA
Gilliland Printing, Arkansas City, Kansas

CONTENTS

PREFACE

Imagine if you were a Pleiadian man or woman living in a Utopian society where peace had reigned for 50,000 years. You would be able to enjoy a life span of 700 to 1200 years of perfect health and infinite possibilities for personal growth. Truth would rule your life as it does your whole society. Everyone is taken care of. There is no poverty, starvation, disease, juvenile delinquency, ecological abuse, or war, and almost no crime or divorce. You have evolved beyond chronic negative thinking. You can telepathically communicate with your friends and loved ones wherever they might be in the universe. Your starships can travel anywhere and to any time period—past, present, or future. Your race has mastered the universe. And you are propelled by your unbounded love to share your good fortune with others. So you try, again and again, to guide less developed races of humans in the Milky Way galaxy to grow and evolve spiritually. Now, in the twentieth century, you try to help the warring peoples of planet Earth turn to the Truth and to change their self-destructive ways and evolve into a peaceful and loving society.

Such is the case, and herein lies the tale of that effort by the Pleiadians to help Earth humanity awaken to true spirituality. Gene Andrade's *Star Wisdom* is a great experience in the discovery of higher consciousness. Read on to learn of the real truths about life and death, God and man, and religion and spirituality.

—*Randolph Winters*
November 5, 1995

INTRODUCTION

On January 28, 1975, a Swiss farmer by the name of Eduard Albert (Billy) Meier was contacted by extraterrestrial humans from the star system we call "The Pleiades." (Actually, they explained that they were from a star system in the area of the Pleiades but in a dimension one/half second different from ours). They met with him and took him aboard their starships for a wondrous journey throughout our universe. They taught him their viewpoints about life and shared with him their teachings on religion and spirituality. They allowed him to photograph and even to film their beamships ("flying saucers") so that people would believe Billy was truly having contacts with extraterrestrials. But when Billy Meier offered this photographic proof to the world, he was denounced, harassed, and ridiculed—and many attempts were even made to assassinate him.

Thus, the world let the Pleiadians know that Earth-humans were not ready to change their old ways. The Pleiadians stopped their contacts with Billy, telling him that it would probably take many centuries before the mass of humanity would be ready to accept extraterrestrial contact with such an advanced race as the Pleiadians. They said, however, that even now a few humans could be reached with the liberating teachings that they were giving Billy. And as this teaching from the stars spreads slowly through Earth society, we can eventually learn how to create a loving, peaceful, harmonious civilization like theirs.

Much of the information that the Pleiadians gave to Billy has been published by Lt. Col. Wendelle C. Stevens (Ret.): in *UFO Contact from the Pleiades—a Preliminary Investigation Report, UFO Contact from the Pleiades—a Supplementary*

Investigation Report, and *Message from the Pleiades—*
The Contact Notes of Eduard Billy Meier (Books 1 and 2).
(The original *Contact Notes* are 1,800 pages describing
all that transpired between Billy and the Pleiadians during
his many meetings with them over a three-year period).
Randolph Winters has published an excellent overall
compilation of the Pleiadian material, entitled *The Pleiadian
Mission—a Time of Awareness.* He also has available a won-
derfully informative 16-cassette tape series of lectures about
the *Contact Notes* and other books of Billy Meier. Gary
Kinder has written a very objective book, called *Light Years,*
which describes his journalistic investigation of Billy Meier.

Genesis Publications has made available to the public
all the videotapes of the Pleiadian beamships in three videocassettes called *The Beamship Trilogy.* Randolph Winters also
has a video, *The Pleiadian Connection,* which is an excellent
introduction to the Pleiadian material and which contains
many of the best slides of the beamships.

Because of the abundance of books, videos, and
cassettes available describing the Pleiadians and their
contacts with Billy, I won't repeat that information but
instead will discuss some of the basic principles of spirituality that the Pleiadians have offered humanity and how
they differ from present-day Earth beliefs. This book is a
presentation of my own beliefs. I am in no way affiliated
with Billy Meier, or any group, religion, or any other
organization. I offer these ideas of mine in the hope that
they will encourage new and creative thinking in the
reader and that these transcendent and liberating spiritual
principles will help bring about a better world.

—*Gene Andrade*

STAR WISDOM

Principles of Pleiadian Spirituality

Part I

The Basics of Pleiadian Spirituality

Billy Meier has revealed to the world a body of information that could greatly change our beliefs and replace them with a philosophy of truth that opens the mind and facilitates true spiritual growth. The spirituality of the Pleiadians has seven basic principles: Oneness, Eternal Spiritual Evolution, Self-Responsibility, Love, Balance, Truth, and Equality. It is this philosophy that I believe will eventually become the basis of spirituality for Earth humanity. It is by applying these principles to your life that you will discover their validity and importance. Reflecting upon these seven essential factors of Pleiadian spirituality will enable you to realize how cosmic, how universal in scope, how liberating is this perspective as compared with the ordinary earthly religious way of seeing life.

CHAPTER ONE

ONENESS AND ETERNAL EVOLUTION OF SPIRIT

What is Pleiadian spirituality? It is the philosophy of life that the advanced extraterrestrials from the Pleiades follow. In their culture there are no religions such as on Earth. What Pleiadians use as their guiding principles are the natural laws of Creation that they have thus far discovered. "Creation" is the word they use to designate the Oneness—the magnificent, all-powerful, omniscient force of intelligence, wisdom, and love that has created and is sustaining the universe and all that exists therein. The Pleiadians claim that these principles are scientific fact, not blind beliefs or imagined fantasies of any one person. They refer to our "cult-like religions," saying that our primitive religious beliefs are holding us back from evolving spiritually. With the Pleiadians and other evolved extraterrestrial races, science and spirituality are one—there is no conflict between the two because their spiritual beliefs are based on reality, on fact, rather than some person's opinion about reality.

The Creation

The Pleiadians explained to Billy that the whole universe is the manifestation of what they call "the Creation." This material manifestation of Creation is created to provide an arena for an infinite variety of experiences so that Creation can grow in knowledge and wisdom. Life is Creation's dream of oneness. All comes from this one intelligence, this one force that people have labeled as "God."

Actually, the word "God," according to the Pleiadians, is an old Earth word for the Pleiadian leader who was governing the planet Earth about 11,000 years ago. That leader, who was named Jehovan, was an evil-minded despot who deceived the Earthhumans by telling them that he had created them and that he was their master. Jehovan had achieved his position of world leader by murdering his own father, Arus, another very tyrannical and war-like Pleiadian leader of Earth. So the original concept of God comes from a time when mankind was dominated by a tyrannical dictator who wanted the Earth people to be obedient slaves. And what better way to ensure their unquestioning obedience than to create a religion that deified the despotic ruler who was governing them?

Creation is what we ignorantly personify as "God." There is only one force in the universe, and that is Creation. The idea that there are two forces—God and Satan—is an invention of man and is totally false. Creation is one, not two— nor three, as some Hindus believe. The creating, sustaining, and destroying aspects of life are all aspects of the one Creation, not three separate forces, as depicted by the Hindu gods Brahma, Vishnu, and Shiva. The more discerning Hindus see reality as oneness even while simultaneously entertaining the construct of threeness. Pleiadians, though, see only oneness. They do not spiritualize—or institutionalize—the principles of twoness or threeness, even though these principles are operative throughout the universe. Actually, the Pleiadians do not acknowledge any creator. They say that there is Creation, but no creator. This unimaginably magnificent force that has created life is Creation, and all that exists is one with it. There is no separate part of Creation known as "the Creator."

Even though the Pleiadians are vastly more spiritually evolved and technically advanced than mankind, they still do not know the answers to ultimate questions such as: why is there existence?, why does Creation want or need an infinite amount of experiences?, why go through all these stages to evolve into beings of light and love instead of just starting at that level? They are as ignorant as we are in terms of these basic questions. Maybe the truth is as the Hindu mystics proclaim: God (Creation) was bored and so created the universe as a divine play for self-amusement. Maybe the ultimate knowledge is unknowable. Or maybe when we evolve into light beings then we will fully understand the purpose of life, and all questions will be answered.

The Pleiadians claim that there are 10^{49} universes, but they have personally only visited one other universe— a parallel one called the DAL Universe. The all-powerful force, the infinite, intelligent energy that creates universes, has created, is maintaining, and will dissolve our universe. The cycle of creating and then dissolving the universe is called a "Greattime" and lasts about 311 trillion years. These Greattimes alternate with sleeptimes of equal duration in which there is no material manifestation of Creation. The Hindu texts, called the Upanishads, speak of these seven great days and nights of the universe in which material manifestation of the universe alternates with absolute emptiness. (In addition to the Upanishads, the Pleiadians say that the Mayan calender, the Kabbala, and the Talmud of Jmmanuel are the spiritual teachings on Earth that are most valid.) Seven cycles of Greattimes is called an Eternity, and that constitutes the evolutionary process by which a Creation graduates to a higher level and becomes a UR Universe. It then acts as the force that creates more universes. And then that UR Universe, after seven cycles of creating universes, goes on to become a Central Universe. The Pleiadians say they don't fully understand what a Central Universe does.

The universe that we live in is in the second of the seven cycles of Greattimes, and 47 trillion years have passed so far in that 311 trillion year cycle. (These figures are vastly greater than what present day Earth scientists say is the age of the universe.) Thus there is plenty of time for an infinite number of experiences when you consider that the whole cycle of seven Greattimes amounts to roughly 15 quad-rillion years. That is 15,000,000,000,000,000 years!

Reincarnation

The basic principle of evolution is that human beings reincarnate over and over again into the material plane so that they can have experiences that enable them to learn life's lessons and thereby evolve into beings of higher con-sciousness and greater love.

According to the Pleiadians, there are actually two meanings to the word evolution. The first meaning is a development and unfolding of what already exists but is hidden. Spiritually this means that something has to rise from the unconscious to the conscious. The second meaning is that something that does not yet exist is created, developed, and explored.

Each human has a spirit that never dies. The physical body dies but the spirit that inhabits the body is immortal; birth and death are simply the spirit's entrance into, and exit from, the material plane. At death, the spirit goes into the fine-matter realm. The soul, or spirit, is bound to the fine-matter realm that is connected to the planet where the person died. Thus, all persons who die on Earth reincarnate as humans on the Earth. If a Pleiadian spacecraft crashed on Earth and the beings on board all died, all of them would reincarnate on Earth as Earthhumans. For someone to reincarnate as a Pleiadian on their home planet Erra (which revolves around a star called Taygeta—but in a slightly different dimension than the one we are in), that person has to die on the planet Erra. So, we humans are bound to this planet Earth. And if we want to live and incarnate into a spiritually advanced civilization like that of the Pleiadians, then we have to create such a society here on this world.

People reincarnate as people, never as animals or plants. Animals do not evolve spiritually as do humans. Rather, they are part of an overall evolution of nature itself.

The Earth itself is a creature and undergoes its own evolution. It goes through a sleep and a waking cycle. Its sleep cycle manifests as a glacial period in which a large part of the land mass is covered with a thick layer of ice. During that period of time, which comes regularly, plants and animals have to adapt to the changing conditions and therefore they evolve into new and higher forms. An example of that is the elephant, which evolved from the mammoth during a previous glacial period. It lost its shaggy coat, its tusks changed their shape, and its intelligence increased. Then it migrated to warmer climates from the cold regions it had previously inhabited.

The average age of a typical Earthhuman spirit, according to the Pleiadians, is about 100 million years. And they say that we have to incarnate on a material planet like Earth for approximately 60 to 80 *billion* years before we evolve beyond the need for a physical body. When we do evolve to that stage, then we exist just as light bodies, as centers of consciousness that eventually unite as group souls of seven spirits. Then, over great lengths of time, all the group souls unite into oneness and the whole universe passes out of that stage, becoming a higher type of universe that creates other universes. After that, there is yet more spiritual evolvement. And on and on it goes.

This grand process of evolvement into a state of pure light and love, into a state of indescribable oneness, has seven growth cycles, each of which has seven stages. (See Appendix No.2)

The essential Pleiadian message in regard to spiritual evolvement is that we grow and grow and grow, with no end point ever (at least that they know of). Thus, there is no "enlightenment" as many of Earth's spiritual teachings have conceptualized it. There is no transcending of mundane life and then just disappearing into nothingness or into a state of blissful oneness in which we do nothing but vegetate in our bliss. While there is transcendence into being pure light and love, we still learn and grow and relate to others, even though we then exist as light beings (centers of consciousness with no material body).

And the higher a spirit evolves, the more it takes on the task of guiding and serving other less evolved spirits. What a wonderful destiny, for service to others is one of the most satisfying endeavors in life. When we experience our true being, we feel bliss. When we bring ourselves into alignment with Creation by surrendering to the Truth, we feel peace. And when we serve Creation by helping others, then we feel unlimited joy.

CHAPTER TWO

SELF-RESPONSIBILITY

Your spiritual evolvement is totally your own personal responsibility. To assume that someone else such as God or a guru is going to do it for you is erroneous. In fact, it is only when you do accept personal responsibility that you start growing spiritually.

What we have on Earth are cults. Some are very large, which we call world religions—and some are small, which we simply label as cults. But most all of them are based on worshipping an individual, whom we regard as Divine, as one with God, the creator and ruler of all that is—or else as the messenger of God. And as the basic teaching of these individuals gets changed over the centuries, the resultant belief system gets further and further from the truth. The Pleiadians say that religions are not all bad, for they do contain much truth. Too often, though, the truth is sandwiched between lies and thus the religion prevents real spiritual development.

The original founder of a religion might simply have been expounding the basic truths of life; but after his death, the religious and political leaders would often twist his teachings so as to create a mythology that would maintain the priestly and political hierarchy. Their aim was not to serve the Truth, but to serve their egos and to keep people in a subservient, docile state and to maintain themselves as the rulers and leaders of society. Cult leaders don't want their followers to think and act for themselves, to be independent, self-empowered, autonomous followers of their own inner light. They want people to be frightened sheep who can be controlled, manipulated, and exploited.

What leads people to get caught up in cults? I believe that it is the unconscious desire of the individual follower to abdicate self-responsibility and to have someone else take responsibility for his life. We want a sense of security and are willing to do anything or believe in anything in order to have this sense that there is some powerful authority figure (god or guru) looking out for us.

The Pleiadians believe in self-responsibility and in the benevolent force of life itself. Their "God" is Creation. They seek to understand the laws of Creation by observing and studying nature. And it is by obeying the laws of Creation that they have evolved into such a loving, harmonious, peaceful race. Their "religion" is the knowledge of life, the understanding of the nature of the universe, and the thorough comprehension of how and why reality functions as it does. They understand birth, life, and death. And this understanding guides their lives and their society.

Self-reliance

The Pleiadians told Billy Meier that any Earthhumans who wanted to be contacted by them had to first reach the spiritual level where they could solve life problems completely by themselves without recourse to teachers or books. In other words, they had to have adopted a life attitude of total self-responsibility and self-reliance. The Pleiadians found that if they contacted humans who were not yet sufficiently evolved spiritually, then inevitably the Earthhumans ended up worshipping the Pleiadians as gods. They don't want that to happen again and so they have disseminated their message of truth and love through Billy Meier, who they say wouldn't fall into the trap of idolizing them. In the ancient past they showed themselves to large numbers of people in order to help humanity develop certain forms of thinking. But people were so awed by the technical wizardry of the Pleiadians and other extraterrestrials that they began to believe in miracles. This led them astray spiritually because it fostered abdication of personal responsibility and worshipping of the ETs as gods. Now is not the time for irrefutable visible proofs—for a mass public landing of beamships. Now is the time for the development of clear, rational, and logical thinking on the part of Earth humanity.

Looking around us, we can observe that most people would rather have someone else solve their problems. In fact, the vast majority of people on this planet look not to their own self for guidance but to a god figure, priests, gurus, and spiritual teachers. And the result is that the blind lead the blind. Not only that, but everyone practices denial of what they are really doing, which is the abdication of self-responsibility and the giving away of one's personal power to another.

Why do we do that? I believe it is because we are afraid of life and we desperately want to avoid feeling our insecurity. Instead of embracing our weakness and befriending those feelings, thereby learning from them and growing truly strong, we run from our feelings of insecurity and do anything we can to cover them over and create the illusion in our minds that everything is all right and we are secure. So we have a hidden agenda. When we are ostensibly seeking the truth through spiritual pursuits, we often are actually trying to flee from our feelings of insecurity and low self-esteem and from unresolved emotional problems. This makes us easy prey for religious authorities to exploit us.

This unconscious avoidance of one's reality and the desperate seeking of an answer to life's uncertainty makes one vulnerable to exploitation by certain cults, gurus, and religions. In fact, cults usually target such people. The person who is running from himself is already primed for indoctrination by a cult because he has this hidden agenda which a guru (or anyone who has studied himself and others) can easily perceive. The guru, seeing the person's insecurity and the hidden desire to avoid dealing with it, easily captures the person by promising salvation, eternal security, divine protection, and unconditional acceptance. "Rely on me," says the guru, "and you will have no more worries." And no more need to take responsibility for yourself. A most attractive message to one who is fleeing from himself. Unfortunately, the truth of life is that one must develop oneself and grow and learn and evolve in one's own being. To assume that another will do that for you is self-deceptive and self-defeating.

Gurus and Cults

So that there will be no misunderstanding, I want to make it clear that when I use the word "guru," I am describing power-oriented spiritual leaders who use, abuse, and exploit their followers. I am not condemning the potentially beneficial relationship of a spiritual student with a highly-evolved teacher who treats others with dignity, respect, and integrity. Such a relationship is a rare blessing that can greatly aid one's spiritual evolution. Historically, there are accounts of guru-disciple relationships in which one person helped another to grow spiritually without any sort of abusiveness or exploitation. Unfortunately, such cases seem quite rare nowadays. When our spiritual leaders fully embody these Pleiadian principles of spirituality, then they will be competent to teach spirituality. Until then, look very closely at any teacher or teachings you follow.

It is imperative that you look to your inner teacher, to your own heart, for guidance and help in discerning what to do and how to grow spiritually. While it can be beneficial to learn from another who functions as a spiritual guide, it is important not to give away your personal power to your teacher. You can discern the bona fide spiritual teachers by whether or not they welcome and encourage you to leave them and to pursue your own personal path of evolution. If you are not perfectly free to leave your teacher whenever you want, then you need to ask yourself if you are in a cult.

Combating Cult Mind Control, by Steven Hassan, is one of the best books on the subject of cults and their insidious methods of mind control. It tells you exactly the kind of questions to ask yourself in determining if a group is a destructive cult. In its detailed presentation of the sophisticated techniques that destructive cults use to gain control over unsuspecting people, it exposes exactly how a cult exploits its members, turning them into dependent automatons. Describing the characteristics of mind control, the criteria of a destructive cult, and the basics of cult psychology, Hassan goes on to explain how exit-counseling helps free someone from the bondage of mind control.

Systematically using modern psychological mind control techniques to break members down and undermine their self-esteem, cunning cult leaders gain control over their victims' thoughts, emotions, and behavior. Anyone, absolutely anyone, can become a victim of cult indoctrination. Forewarned is forearmed.

One key point that Hassan makes is that people do not join cults. Rather, cults recruit and entrap people, usually at a most vulnerable time in their life, through deception and intimidation. And once in a cult, the member is indoctrinated so as to be phobic about ever leaving the group. Through step-by-step mind control techniques, people can even be made to believe that they will die if they leave, or a nuclear war will start if they are disloyal to the guru and leave the cult. They become enslaved by the clever and unscrupulous cult leader.

Cults are very successful in undermining one's ability to make personal decisions and in reducing one to the state of a dependent adolescent. They disrupt the individual's identity and supplant it with one of their own making—one that is totally subservient to the leader's will. The cult member is taught to believe the leader, and definitely not to follow their own logic or reason. Cults do not want people who think for themselves.

To free someone from bondage to a cult, "Exit-counselors" help the person to connect again with their pre-cult identity, with their previous hopes and ambitions and persona. The Exit-counselor helps the member grow and mature as a person, naturally leading them to leave the cult. By getting the member to be honest, to really feel how unhappy they are in the cult, to question the thoughts and feelings they had previously denied and suppressed, cult members begin to connect with their real self and to understand how they have been tricked into giving up their individuality and autonomy. The new perspective given them by the counselor enables them to free themselves from the mind-control spell they have been under. Only then, when they take personal responsibility for their life, can they have freedom and genuine spiritual growth.

Another excellent book that describes the dynamics of cults is Arthur Deikman's *The Wrong Way Home—Uncovering the Patterns of Cult Behavior in American Society*. He explains how cults exploit their followers, rationalize the impropriety of the guru, suppress rational-critical thinking, and appeal to the baser instincts (fear, greed, flattery, etc.) in order to capture new members. Cults attract people who are looking for parent-substitutes, for wise and powerful guardians who promise them guidance, love, and security. Cults enable people to act out their dependency wishes. Some of the issues this book deals with are dependency on a leader, compliance with the group, devaluing outsiders, and avoiding dissent. Anyone can be vulnerable to the allure of cults. This is so because we all want to be loved, feel secure, and to live meaningful lives—and cults promise to deliver all of that if you will only surrender to the guru.

The surrendering of one's personal power is not only detrimental to oneself—it is also harmful to the guru. Joel Kramer and Diana Alstad have eloquently described the dangers and follies of the guru-disciple relationship in their book, *The Guru Papers—Masks of Authoritarian Power*. They make the interesting point that the very nature of the guru-disciple relationship creates a social structure that is almost guaranteed to corrupt the guru.

Corrupt Spiritual Teachers

Spiritual leaders/religious teachers become corrupt so easily because of many factors. Their belief systems are often illogical and irrational and are not aligned with the truth of Creation, because they were created not to enlighten the followers, but to perpetuate a power structure. The leaders are exposed to unceasing adulation from large numbers of followers for decades, which feeds their egos and enables them to believe they are gods. The guru has to appear as an infallible Knower-of-all-that-is, especially if he claims to be enlightened (and if he wants to keep up with the competition from other gurus who proclaim their infallibility and infinite wisdom). This leads to self-deception since the leader, being human, has to have foibles and weaknesses, and cannot live without making some mistakes. So, when the inevitable occurs and their all-too-human weaknesses and faults surface, the gurus deny them, and then more and more they enter into a path of self-deception, subterfuge, and lies. Being without peers who could offer a form of corrective guidance, the guru spirals down into a pit of self-created folly and usually increasingly bizarre behavior. That is why so many modern gurus have ended up as suicidal megalomaniacs who lead their followers to their death.

These so-called spiritual teachers exhort their flocks to deny their own rationality, common sense, and self-reliance and to instead blindly submit to the guru. This they term "surrender to the Divine." If you resist, you are told that you are full of ego, you are "in your head," you are resisting the will of God, you are on the path to damnation, etc., etc.

All the possible mind-control techniques and forms of manipulation used in the name of goodness and God are really just the shoddy antics of con men trying to get you to abdicate your own personal power and common sense intelligence. If you remain in your power and see the reality of the situation, they can't so easily deceive and exploit you.

To counter that self-reliance, religions have exhorted their followers to be meek and submissive. They say that the meek will inherit the earth. And the reason they say that is because they want you to be meek and docile in order to easily control you.

Spiritual teachers often have hidden agendas (such as getting rich by financially exploiting you). Best to regard them and their organizations as existing to serve you. Keep in mind that many so-called spiritual teachers will do their best to turn that attitude around and get you to believe that you exist only to serve them! They will phrase it in terms such as, "Serve these teachings of Truth and help liberate others," or "Help this wonderful organization that is spreading the only true teachings of Liberation and is making people happy," etc.

Most spiritual teachings are a mixture of truth and falseness. If you can't discern what is the false part you will probably end up getting hurt by it. Think for yourself and never ever give your power away to anybody or any organization, no matter how holy they proclaim themselves to be. Always ask, "Is this really serving me"? If it isn't, abandon it—don't abandon yourself.

Humanity desperately needs genuine spiritual guidance, and that is why the Pleiadians have contacted us through Billy Meier. They are not our teachers or gurus and are not to be worshipped or made into authority figures. They have simply pointed out to us some of the basics of universal spirituality, and now it is our responsibility to apply these teachings to our daily lives.

Each of us has to do the work of growing up and evolving into the being of light and love that is our true nature. We will return to our Source, but each individual will return with their own self-learned knowledge and hard-earned wisdom. Life is to be lived, and we each must accept complete responsibility for our own life if we are to grow spiritually. That doesn't mean that we can't learn from someone who temporarily functions as a teacher of spiritual truths, but it does mean that we must not make the teacher into an authority figure, because that hinders our evolution.

And we must see through the illusion that some people are "enlightened" and others are not. The belief that a human being can reach the end point of evolution and learning is completely false. People who claim to have achieved total self-knowledge and to have finished the spiritual evolution process are deluding themselves. We always are learning and growing. A teacher who proclaims himself to be enlightened is like a man drawing a line in the sand and declaring that he is on the right side of the line and is therefore enlightened! And then he tells you that because you are on the opposite side of this arbitrarily drawn line you need to follow him!

Pleiadians say that there is no such thing as a spiritual hierarchy of ascended masters. Some so-called masters, such as Saint Germain, were charlatans and con-men. In any case, they possess no special powers, and to ascribe magical powers to them only serves to disempower yourself.

The Pleiadians describe us as a race held in bondage by our cult-like religions. And since their ancestors were responsible for creating the type of authoritarian and dogmatic religions now governing Earth, they are trying to rectify that mistake by introducing mankind to the true principles of spirituality, so we can evolve into a harmonious and happy society.

A word of warning: the author strongly cautions the reader to beware of joining any UFO group, even one dealing with the Pleiadian material. At this time in Earth society's evolution, it is almost inevitable that such groups are, or will become, cults. It is probably better to simply study the material on your own or together with your partner and perhaps a few close friends.

CHAPTER THREE

LOVE

For the Pleiadians, love is not a word or an idea, but a way of life. Their whole culture is based upon love. And justice. Their love is not some emotionally unbalanced, maudlin attitude that is based on fantasy, but is an expression of their natural attunement to Creation. Having harmonized themselves with life, they act with a love that is balanced, mature, intelligent, and wise.

Semjase (pronounced Sem-yah-see), the Pleiadian woman who met with Billy Meier more than one hundred times, always acted lovingly and compassionately towards him. And every time Billy met Asket, the extraterrestrial from the parallel DAL Universe who contacted him repeatedly when he was a young man, he felt a wave of blissful love emanate from her that would just envelop and overwhelm him. She could extend her being to him as pure love and that would fill his heart. [Please see Randolph Winters' or Wendelle Stevens' books for more information on Asket.]

The Decalogue

It is by understanding and following Creational laws that one is able to truly love oneself, others, and Creation itself. The Pleiadian High Council enabled Billy to receive transmissions of the Creational laws from a very highly evolved group-spirit called Petale. This information was translated into English and published in America in 1987 under the title, *The Decalogue*. Here is my paraphrase of the 12 laws of Creation:

1. Have no authority figures, gods, or idols except Creation.
2. Honor the name of Creation.
3. Make of each day a holy day.
4. Honor your connection with Creation.
5. Honor Creation as you would honor your parents.
6. Honor life and don't needlessly kill.
7. Respect the property and rights of others.
8. Honor the truth.
9. Speak the truth.
10. Accept your life with gratitude and don't be greedy for that which your neighbor possesses.
11. Accept the truth and don't disparage the truth.
12. Honor and obey Creation's laws and never place these laws into cults and religions.

All twelve of these laws were given to Moses, but only the first ten were incorporated into the religion of that time. And those ten were presented as the following ten commandments:

1. I am the Lord thy God. Thou shalt have no other gods before me.
2. Thou shalt not make unto thee any graven image.
3. Thou shalt not take the name of the Lord thy God in vain.
4. Remember the Sabbath day and keep it holy.
5. Honor thy father and thy mother.
6. Thou shalt not kill.
7. Thou shalt not commit adultery.
8. Thou shalt not steal.

9. Thou shalt not bear false witness against thy neighbor.
10. Thou shalt not covet your neighbor's goods.

Notice how the laws of the former list are positive and cosmic in nature and serve to empower the individual and bring him into alignment with Creation, while the laws of the latter list are negative and very worldly and serve to disempower the individual and to make him frightened of some vengeful "God".

The Decalogue could be summarized as follows: Love yourself, love others, and love Creation; be true to yourself, be true to others, and be true to Creation.

The Pleiadians accept life in the physical plane and so they have no neurotic hang-ups about all the different aspects of material life, including sex and romance. Here, paraphrased in my own words, is the essence of what Semjase has said about physical and emotional love.

Religious fanatics tend to imagine that sexuality is bad, immoral, and degenerate. Their foolish delusions prevent them from seeing that Creation itself has mandated this type of repro-duction and that throughout the universe sexuality has proven to be a good and positive aspect of life. It is not unspiritual or impure. Sexual reproduction is natural and normal.

Mary, the mother of Jmmanuel, was impregnated by Gabriel, a Pleiadian man. It is a fantasy to believe that Jmmanuel was conceived by any spiritual power or by the "Holy Spirit." Gabriel fathered Jmmanuel because those who were governing some of the Earthly human races at that time wanted him to do so. The leader of the governing group was an IHWH, or as the Earthhumans called him, a god. [Author: IHWH stands for

"Ishwish," which is a word meaning "King of Wisdom."
See Appendix No. 2, Step 5, Level 6 for more information.]
*They needed Mary to couple with a highly advanced being like
Gabriel so that they could create an adequate vehicle for the
incarnation of Jmmanuel. There were no Earth men who were
evolved enough to be able to supply the right DNA, etc. for creat-
ing a body that could house such a supremely evolved spirit as
Jmmanuel's. So they chose a Pleiadian father to mate with Mary.
The Pleiadians tell us that Joseph, understandably, was not
pleased with this arrangement. However, when Gabriel explained
the whole situation to him, Joseph accepted it and married
Mary even though she was then pregnant with Gabriel's child,
Jmmanuel.*

*The false ideas that sex is somehow sinful or evil arose when
ancient religious leaders tried to control the sexuality of the
primitive Earthhumans by telling them numerous lies about sex
in the hopes that that would curb the excessive and degenerate
sexual habits prevalent then. They didn't realize how much sexual confusion and delusion those false teachings would create for
future generations.*

*Pleiadians love one another with all their feelings just as do
Earthhumans. But Pleiadians form only monogamous marriages
and then only after thorough clarification that both partners are
truly suited to each other. Therefore, our marriages last for a
lifetime, and divorce is an extremely rare occurrence. Divorce as
you know it is not allowed with us. Only if a partner dies or is
exiled for life for some heinous crime does a marriage get dis-
solved and the remaining partner allowed to remarry. Our laws
regarding matrimony and intercourse have remained the same
for millennia and are corresponding to those outlined in* The
Talmud of Jmmanuel. [Author: An English translation of
this book, purported to be the only true presentation of

Jmmanuel's teachings written during his lifetime, was published in 1992.] *What has changed for us is that we practice a more humane form of punishment in matters of serious criminal behavior. The uniform penalty for breaking laws in these matters is lifelong exile to a penal planet where only men or only women live. There they live out their lives in isolation from the rest of our race and are denied technological comforts.* [Author: They are, however, given spiritual material to study in hopes that that will enable them to truly change.]

Our High Council decides how many births are to be allowed in any time period so that our race is preserved while not creating a situation of overpopulation. On my home planet, Erra, we have about 500 million people. Since Earth is of almost identical size as Erra, you too should limit your population to approximately half a billion people. It is a natural obligation of each form of life to create descendants so the species is preserved. But it is also the obligation that the population be controlled.

Pleiadian women have technical means of determining if they are pregnant within three days of insemination. If the pregnancy is undesired, they use a natural preparation to induce an early menstruation, which then serves to expel the ovum before it is able to develop. A spirit inhabits a fertilized egg three weeks after procreation. Inducing menstruation up to that time period results only in the expulsion of basic elements and substances from the woman and no spirit is killed. Except in emergency cases in which a woman's life is endangered by the fetus, no aborting procedures are allowed after three weeks from the date of fertilization. To do so would be against natural law. When Pleiadian women do carry a baby to term, which takes nine months, they then give birth naturally, without the use of any pain medication.

*While Pleiadians are sexually able to procreate at 10 1/2
years of age, they practice continence until they are at least 70
years old.* [Author: Since they have lifespans of 700 to 1200
years, that initial period of continence is, relatively speak-
ing, quite short.] *During that time they concentrate on their
education and spiritual studies. They do not stop learning at that
age but continue their whole life to learn and grow spiritually.*

*Unlike the way Earthhumans love one another, our way of
loving one another is very pure, deep, constant, and long-last-
ing. Of course, in a marriage there are differences of opinion
but these do not degenerate into fights. Such differences between
the two partners serves their evolution and is essential for their
growth. It is an irrevocable law of evolution that there be some
differences between the man and woman so that the ensuing conflict can stimulate change and spiritual growth.*

[Author: more on love and marriage in Chapter 4.]

*One who is filled with love is also rich in wisdom, and one
who is rich in wisdom is also full of love. Earthhumans deceive
themselves, for they do not know love. They think that feelings
of possessive desire are love.*

*You become a real human being when you realize the truth,
the knowledge, and the wisdom even if you do not use the word
"Creation." Love in its best form is wisdom. So the human being
always discovers that understanding and enlightenment are also
wisdom and love, and where love rules, there also rules wisdom.*

*If Earthhumans would only love one another, your planet
would be a paradise.*

Hyperspace Experience

One of the ways that the Pleiadians educate their people is by giving them the direct, personal experience of Oneness and Infinite Love so that each individual has the true knowledge born of real experience of what life is actually about. They do this by allowing their citizens to fly on a journey in one of their spacecraft as it goes into hyperspace. When a Pleiadian spacecraft traverses immense distances of millions of light years, it does so in a fraction of a second by going into a null-time/null-space dimension, which they call "hyperspace." They use a light-emitting drive to accelerate up to the speed of light. Then, just at the moment of equaling the speed of light, they shut off the protective energy field surrounding their craft and use the resulting force of the implosion to somehow go into a dimension of no-time/no-space. Then, by using their advanced technology, they can instantly reappear anywhere in the universe.

While in this hyperspace state of being, one experiences pure spirit. That is, one experiences oneself as bodiless and has the incredibly blissful realization of one's true spiritual identity—as being undying spirit and not just a physical body. This ecstatic realization of Oneness, of being one with All That Is, is the Self-realization experience so sought after by mystics throughout history. The experience of hyperspace can be extended to last seven minutes before the beamship has to rematerialize into the physical plane. The Pleiadians let Billy Meier have this experience that is so integral to the Pleiadian education of their young. Billy spoke at great length of this experience in the *Contact Notes*, which were transliterated from German into English. Even though the transliteration was extremely difficult to understand (as the translator had given a word-by-word and not necessarily grammatical, translation), I have tried to present a more readable paraphrase of Billy's seven-minute experience in hyperspace.

At first all I can see is a milky-white mass. All the stars have merged into glowing whiteness everywhere, just like I have seen before on previous hyperleaps when the Pleiadians have taken me on journeys throughout the galaxy. But now as the experience continues, the milky whiteness disappears and all is utter blackness. This time I am being allowed to stay in a hyperspace state for seven minutes. Now what? Everywhere is golden light, a brilliant glowing light that is like all the suns of the universe shining together. And this wondrous light does not hurt the eyes. This is the glistening light of eternity. How utterly magnificent! Wonder of wonders! Only this eternity exists. There is no other than eternity. There is no time. Only this glorious magnificence exists. And what is this? It is love, Love, LOVE! Only love exists. All is love. Oh, what peace, what Love! I exist, and yet I do not exist. This is all so incredible. So full of love, so deep, so profound. Eternity is I, and I am also in eternity. I am a human being, a visitor in the eternity. . . . What now? Only light. I can see nothing but light. But I don't see anything with my eyes—yet I see, and I don't hear with my ears—and yet I hear. Now I know— I am eternity, I am infinite love! I am not a human being! I am beingness. I can feel, I am alive. Even though I do not have my senses, I still exist. And I exist as such peace, such love, such infiniteness. . . . I am being called. Who calls for me? The light! The light is calling me. This is so wonderful that I want to remain here forever. I don't want to be a human being—I don't ever want to leave this deep love. This is true existence. Now I understand who I really am. I am pure existence. This is where I belong. My old life as a human being seems so distant, like a dream. Now I feel like I am eternity itself. Material life is just a dream. Here is reality. And death? Death does not exist. Spirit never dies. Now I am I. No more do I care about material life. This glorious light of love, this wondrous eternity is my home.

And this home is oneness. No more do I perceive the many. Now, only the great unity exists. And I am that. . . . I don't fully understand all this. How can I be thinking of me as ever having been separate from this great wholeness? That way of thinking must have come from my life as a material being. Now I dissolve into pure existence, into eternity, and all that I can feel is wholeness. I am simply consciousness. I am absolute being. I am infinite love. All is calm, all is peace. . . . Why do not people on Earth understand this? Why do they search for love in foolishness, in falseness? Why am I even thinking of that, when I am experiencing such blissful oneness? I understand. Eternity cares for itself. It observes humans and wants them to know the truth of eternalness. But humans are so ignorant of the truth and are so misled by the cultlike religions of Earth. There is no deity figure—there is only love eternal. Religions are delusions that lead man away from the Truth and lead to terrible destruction. Oh, why doesn't man want to grow spiritually and become who he really is—the eternity? And even this level of consciousness that I am now experiencing is not the highest. This is the last step of all spirit levels before the final merging with Creation. And that level of spiritual being is infinitely greater and more magnificent than the level I am now experiencing. This is the level of the last stage of perfection before union with the Creation. This is the step of awareness of self as truly existing in the great-all-oneness. And in this stage of spiritual evolvement one overcomes all separateness, all feelings of me and mine, so that one merges at last with the Source of one's being. One's consciousness is eternity calling one home. It is the call of Truth, of all-fulfilling love. The Creation alone exists, and nothing besides the Creation exists. The Creation is the truth in the universe. The Creation is ever-evolving love and existence. This formless Creation is spiritual consciousness, spiritual love, and perfected spiritual being. How ignorant is man to conceive of gods and elevate them to the level of Creation! If only man would recognize the truth and the ever-present love of Creation, then he too could experience this bliss of

eternity. Man needs to advise himself of the truth and use the
power of his spirit to evolve into this state of blissful oneness. He
must recognize the falseness of all cultic heresies and deities, and
he must recognize the way of truth and all-fulfilling love that
alone leads to union with the magnificence of Creation. Only the
truth that is the real Truth leads to the kingdom of eternity. The
word of Truth is everlasting because it is of the great all-oneness.
Heaven and earth will pass away but the words of truth will
never die. . . . Oh no! The glistening light is going away. The light
is vanishing. [The spaceship is rematerializing into the physical plane] *I don't want to return to being a human again! I*
belong in the light. The light is now golden. And now it is silver.
I don't want to be here. I want to return to that place of all love
and beingness. . . . Now I am back to being me—full of prob-
lems, burdens, sorrows, and needs. Oh, this miserable life, why
have I returned? I could just cry. If only I could leave this mater-
ial realm and return to that realm of light and love!

Billy's experience shows how wonderful it is to know
oneself as pure spirit and what a glorious existence awaits
us as we evolve into the level of spiritual oneness with
Creation. As one evolves spiritually, one can exist on the
material plane and still maintain the awareness of one's true
identity as blissful spirit. Then one lives more and more in
the realm of light and love while inhabiting a physical body.
Gradually, over billions of years of incarnations into the
physical plane, one evolves beyond the need for a physical
body. Then one graduates to the stage of life where one
exists only as a light body—at first, partially material and
partially immaterial—then one exists solely as a light body.
At last, we return to our home where all is light and love.

CHAPTER FOUR

BALANCE and TRUTH

"Balance in all things" could be the motto of the Pleiadians. They strive to maintain balance in all ways—in their own beings, in the way they live their lives, and how they function as a society. They participate in this universe by helping less advanced races to evolve and by using their highly advanced technology and awesome power to maintain order and harmony in certain sectors of space (our solar system seems to be one such area).

Maintaining a "neutral/positive" mental state, Pleiadians avoid excessive negativism or positivism, both of which they view as unbalanced. Staying mentally neutral, along with having an overall loving, positive outlook on life, is their optimum way of being. This equilibrium enables them to function with great clarity and integrity.

If a Pleiadian on Erra persists in negative thinking, it upsets the "mental atmosphere" on the planet. Because the Pleiadians are so telepathic, they can discover just who is creating the negative mental vibrations—and that person is told to change their thinking or to get off the planet! Their race lives on many different worlds, so that is an option.

Pleiadian Society

It is the Pleiadians' honoring of truth and spirituality that is the primary factor in their having such a Utopian society. They have enjoyed peace now for the last 50,000 years. [See Appendix No.1 of this book for a chronology of the

Pleiadian history and their involvement with Earth.] After almost destroying themselves time after time with global civil wars, the Pleiadians finally chose to base their society on spiritual principles. They elected the most highly spiritually evolved beings of their population to be their governing officials. And as a race they decided to surrender all crucial decisions to a much more advanced race of beings in the Andromeda galaxy. That race is one that is partially material and partially non-material, as the Andromedans are now at the evolutionary stage where they are transitioning out of the material plane.

With guidance from such a highly evolved race of people, the Pleiadians have eliminated war from their lives and have been able to achieve great technical mastery over the material plane. They have the capacity to travel anywhere in the universe or even to other universes. They claim to have the ability to travel through time, either to the past or the future. (They say that all time is now. The past is over and cannot be changed but the future is always in flux, so when they travel to the future what they encounter is just one possible future.) They have been able to extend their lifespan from 700 to 1200 years. With the elimination of all diseases, they enjoy perfect health. They have machines that can dematerialize their bodies and rematerialize them somewhere else, just as is done in the *Star Trek* movies and television shows. And that was the way they usually met with Billy. They would dematerialize him when he was in his house and then rematerialize him on board their beamship. Billy loved practical jokes. When a contact would end he often would have Semjase dematerialize him from on board the beamship and then rematerialize him on the ground right in front of one of his friends. This would be quite a shock to the friends to have a laughing Billy sprout up right out of the ground in front of them.

The Pleiadians can also cloak their beamship, causing it to be invisible to others. They have the ability to make any form of matter become transparent. For example, if they want to see through the metal wall of an Earth satellite, they can do so, observing the astronauts inside and all their actions. Machines on board their beamships can locate individuals through identification of their unique brain patterns, scanning the conscious and subconscious parts of anyone's mind. At one of the early contacts, they demonstrated to Billy a machine that would do just that. They tuned in to Francisco Franco, the ruler of Spain, who was dying at that time. The machine showed how Franco's conscious mind was terrified of dying, but his subconscious mind was at peace with death. Semjase explained that Franco's subconscious mind knew that only the body dies and so there was no need to be fearful. But his conscious mind had not learned that spiritual truth and so was fearful and was struggling against dying. The machine also told when he would die. Afterwards Billy sent a letter to a friend revealing that date, which was a week or so away. And Franco did die on that date.

The Pleiadians observe our solar system from a mothership that is 17,182 meters in diameter, housing 143,000 people. (Interestingly enough, in the 1980s, my local newspaper printed two articles within one week about the sighting of a very large planetoid-like object that was only visible through infrared light. Curiously, after these two articles appeared in print, there was never another mention of this phenomenon. Perhaps the object moved in a non-orbital way, showing that it was not a planet but perhaps a mothership? And therefore all future reports of the phenomenon have been censored?) The mothership is a self-sufficient world containing many androids, which do a lot of the maintenance work. Androids are intelligent robots that are part organic and part machine. Even the Pleiadian beam-ships are part organic: each beamship has an organic brain that is tuned to the brain of the individual that is piloting it and can be operated telepathically by the pilot. Pleiadians usually communicate with one another telepathically. They say that we too have the capacity to be telepathic and eventually will communicate in that way.

With their incredible technology the Pleiadians have been able to change the color of their sky! They claim that they have engineered the sky on Erra to be green-colored. We don't know what color their sky was originally, and why or how they did this is not revealed in the *Contact Notes*. Perhaps the reason has something to do with increasing the amount of oxygen in their atmosphere, since they mentioned to Billy Meier that the oxygen level of the air on their mothership was much higher than the oxygen level on the surface of planet Earth. The increased amount of oxygen contributed to their high level of health and to their ability to go for days without need of sleep.

With androids and robots doing most of the menial work and with such an advanced technology that protects them from any harm, the Pleiadians are free to devote their time and energy for creative pursuits and for serving others. On their home world, Erra, (which is a planet that revolves around a star near the one we call Taygeta, in the constellation of the Pleiades, but in a different dimension that is, in their words, a "part second" off of this one), the Pleiadians devote a few hours a day to work and the rest of the time to spiritual, artistic, and scientific pursuits.

Pleiadian Marriage and Parenthood

Pleiadians fall in love and marry and have children just as we do. In the *Contact Notes,* Semjase has emphatically stated that Pleiadians are strictly monogamous. When a Pleiadian man and woman marry, they do so as equals. One does not possess the other. They unite in harmony, love, and understanding—taking joy and delight in each other, and planning their lives by mutual agreement.

A Pleiadian mother has the ability to meditate and contact the incoming spirit that will be born through her. Asking the spirit what it wants to accomplish in its lifetime, she determines how to best raise the child by offering it the training and experiences that will most advantageously serve its lifepath. Thus, a soul that wants to develop musically could from a very early age be exposed to music and receive guidance in that direction, while a soul that wanted to be a scientist would receive a different type of upbringing.

Homosexuality is a symptom of spiritual confusion, according to the Pleiadians. When a spirit is about to incarnate, it programs the DNA of the developing embryo to become either a boy or a girl, depending on which sex it chooses to be. However, if the incoming spirit is confused about which sex it wants to be, this confusion can translate into homosexuality. The Pleiadians say they can detect such a tendency while the person is young—and then educate and counsel the person to help them develop as a normal heterosexual man or woman.

Pleiadians are semi-vegetarians. They eat mostly fruits and vegetables, but sometimes when they feel a need for being more "grounded," they eat a small rabbit-like mammal. Mostly they just eat snacks of small portions, rather than large meals. And they can go for days without any sleep. All in all, they have bodies that are much finer than our dense ones. Also, rather than exercising as we do to keep in shape, Semjase told Billy that they use the power of "right thinking" to maintain their health and fitness.

There must be balance between materialism and spirituality. If at an early age the human gets entangled into material thinking, he can be influenced to have excessive greed for possessions, thereby becoming obsessed by feelings of hate and love. This can lead to viewing other people as possessions that he greedily desires. He then alternates between feelings of love or hate. The Pleiadians have evolved beyond such attitudes and they no longer feel envy or possessiveness towards one another. They say the degree of possessiveness of a culture can be a good measure of its level of evolvement (which tells us quite a bit about our own planet!).

Another critical factor is the subtle influence of thoughts upon people. The Pleiadians tell us that Earth's cult-like religions foster illogical and negative thoughts, and these serve to lessen the lifespan of people. Also, the greater the number of people assembled in one place, such as a large city, the greater can be the negative influence upon the inhabitants' mental state and lifespan. Pleiadians live not in cities but in small family-type dwellings surrounded by beautiful natural settings.

Another gauge of a society's spiritual level is the average length of life of its members. The higher the spiritual level, the longer the life span. Earthhumans used to have a lifespan of a thousand years because their spiritual level was quite high. The Biblical Methusalah lived during that period many, many thousands of years ago. But when Earth people turned to false religions, their spiritual level plummeted and they began living out of harmony with natural law. Consequently, their lifespan decreased tremendously, becoming just a fraction of what it had been. When Earth humanity turns to universal truth and lives again in harmony with Creational law, the average lifespan will increase.

Truth

The Pleiadians honor and love truth, living their lives by the truth. They are more interested in the truth than in being right. Many times Billy showed them that their ideas about him and other Earthhumans were false. In every instance the Pleiadians accepted the correction graciously and humbly changed their way of thinking. They did not resist the truth in order to protect any ego stance. They had fluid minds that could change quickly and they appreciated being corrected and becoming more knowledgeable.

As their society is truth-based, they have consequently developed a technology that gives them extraordinary mastery over this universe. Their way of life works. And it is by aligning themselves with the truth that they have become so spiritually advanced. Peace, happiness, and long life are enjoyed by them in contrast to our short lives of stress and strife. [See Part Two—Semjase Speaks—for further elaboration on the Pleiadian perspective on Truth.]

The *Contact Notes* explain many of Earth's mysteries, such as the origin of the Egyptian pyramids and the elusive Bigfoot/Yeti/Sasquatch; and throughout the contacts, Semjase revealed to Billy many unusual details about our planet. She said we just don't have our facts right about many things. For example, we are in error in regarding Mt. Everest as the highest mountain on Earth. It is the highest mountain measured from sea level, but

Mt. Chimborazo in Ecuador is 2,150 meters higher than Mt. Everest when the measurement is taken from the center of the planet. The Earth is not perfectly spherical, but is slightly elliptical. Thus, Mt. Chimborazo rises from the area where the Earth has a larger diameter than the diameter beneath the Himalayan mountains. Earth scientists mistakenly assume that they can take valid measurements just from the sea level, as if the Earth was perfectly spherical and the sea level was thus constant around the world, which it is not.

Present-day Earth society is baffling to the Pleiadians. They can't understand why we don't take care of one another and why we don't choose to live more sane and balanced lives. The Pleiadians contend that our illogical cult-like religions are primarily to blame for our illogical thinking and much of our self-destructive behavior. Their contact with Billy was in hope that through him they could influence us to turn to the truth and to adopt a more spiritual and loving way of life. They sincerely want us to be more balanced in our hearts and minds and to have a more peaceful and harmonious society.

Truth to the Pleiadians is the very essence of their spirituality. It needs to become the essence of ours, as well. I believe that the following quote, an ancient Vedic hymn, aptly sums up how the Pleiadians view truth:

"I salute the supreme teacher, the Truth, whose nature is bliss, who is the giver of the highest happiness, who is pure wisdom, who is beyond all qualities and infinite like the sky, who is beyond words, who is one and eternal, pure and still, who is beyond all change and phenomena and who is the silent witness to all our thoughts and emotions—I salute Truth, the supreme teacher."

CHAPTER FIVE

EQUALITY

Pleiadians say that because the entire universe is the manifestation of Oneness, all beings are equal, for each one is created by Creation. Every being that exists is a creature born from that Great-All-Oneness. Some beings are more evolved than others, but in essence all are children of Creation. Therefore no one is better than another or lesser than another. It is simply that some spirits are older and have had many more lifetimes of experience and so have gained more wisdom than younger spirits. But they are not "gods" or superbeings that should be worshipped just because they are more evolved.

And neither sex is superior to the other. Women and men are spiritual equals. A soul incarnates sometimes as a man and sometimes as a woman, thereby learning to develop both the masculine and feminine traits and to become a balanced whole.

In Pleiadian society, both sexes are treated equally and there is no discrimination against women as there is here on Earth. The opportunities are equal for either sex. The strengths and weaknesses of each sex are acknowledged and accepted. Women are known to be less suited to extremely hard physical tasks that demand the kind of physical strength that men possess. But women are more sensitive in their communicative abilities and hence are more companionable than males. Pleiadian beamships are chiefly piloted by females. Semjase said that she found it perplexing that there aren't more Earth women piloting commercial aircraft.

She said that the level of evolvement of a culture could be easily assessed by seeing how free the women are to do different physical tasks and how much they are repressed and forbidden to do things that the men are allowed to do.

The social ranking of the individual, if such ranking could even be applied to their society, is according to the spiritual level of the individual. The Pleiadians actually name themselves by their spiritual level. Semjase's name translates as "half way to being an Ishrish" (an Ishrish being a female lord of wisdom, a very highly evolved being who has achieved great spiritual mastery. An Ishwish is a male lord of wisdom.). Semjase's father, Ptaah, is an Ishwish who is the commander of the Pleiadian mothership stationed in our solar system. [These names, Semjase and Ptaah, are not the true Pleiadian names that are used on their home world but are names that the Pleiadians employ when relating to Earthhumans. Semjase told Billy that their actual names were simply too difficult for Earthhumans to pronounce. However, their Pleiadian names do express their spiritual level of attainment.]

Total racial equality exists among the Pleiadians, and this applies not only to different skin colors and facial features but also to humans and non-humans. On a number of occasions, Semjase was accompanied by a human woman from the Vega system who was of the black race. These two ET women related with love and equality. And when non-human races visited the Earth, they too were treated with love, respect, kindness, compassion, and helpfulness from the Pleiadians. Humanity has to learn that all beings, of whatever form, are beings of Creation and so should be treated with all the love and respect that one would afford Creation itself.

Humans did not come from the apes; rather, the apes came from the humans. Ancient Lyrians experimented on humans, cross-breeding them with animals. A few of these genetic experiments created the Yeti, Sasquatch, and other apes. Intermediate mutations between the human beings and apes created what Earth scientists call Neanderthals, Peking-Man, Africanus, etc. From the very beginning, humans were especially designed by Creation and were destined to be the form that they are.

When later Pleiadians came to Earth and mated with the descendants of their forefathers' experiments, they called the offspring of those unions, "evas" and "adams," meaning respectively, the "bearer"and "Earth human being."

When the Pleiadians decided to leave Earth 2,000 years ago, they called upon a very advanced spirit from a distant planet called Lahson to incarnate upon Earth and to be a prophet of truth to Earth humanity. Traveling to that planet, they asked for a volunteer to come to Earth as a teacher of true spirituality. They said that after a certain number of incarnations on Earth, they would return that spirit to Lahson. At that time, Lahson was populated by "collective consciousnesses" (groups of seven souls that had bonded together in a form called "collective consciousness"). All the Lahson spirits had evolved beyond the need for physical bodies and so were existing only in the fine-matter or spirit world. Each spirit retained some individuality while simultaneously functioning in a group unit. One of the souls of one group volunteered to be a messenger of truth for Earth. With their great spiritual knowledge and advanced technology, the Pleiadians were able to transport that soul out of that fine-matter realm into this plane of existence and then take it to Earth. They were also able to control when and where it would incarnate. Randolph Winters describes all of this in wonderful detail in his book, *The Pleiadian Mission.*

This spirit incarnated on Earth as Jmmanuel, whose name means "the one with divine knowledge." (Centuries after his death, the Earthly religious authorities, anxious to create a dogmatic mythology by which they could control the masses, changed his name to Jesus Christ and altered his teachings to promote an enslaving dogma that replaced the liberating teachings of Jmmanuel.) Gabriel, the "archangel" father of Jmmanuel, was a Pleiadian man. The *Contact Notes* infer that Mary was impregnated naturally, not by artificial insemination. They stress that artificial insemination is not a safe or recommended practice because it promotes genetic mutations. The Pleiadians guided and protected Jmmanuel during his youth and eventually directly contacted him and took him up in their beamship for forty days and forty nights to educate him for his mission. While on board the beamship they used a device to mechanically awaken Jmmanuel's psychic powers, thus enabling him to perform the many miracles mentioned in the Bible. All of this is covered in much greater detail in Randolph Winters' book and in his cassette series, *UFO—The Pleiadian Contacts.*

The Talmud of Jmmanuel

The true teachings of Jmmanuel were discovered in 1963 when the Pleiadians guided a Greek Catholic priest named Isa Rashid to the tomb of Jmmanuel/Jesus Christ in Jerusalem. There he unearthed an ancient text, encased in resin, that was written in ancient Aramaic by Judas Iscariot. The document has been translated into English and published as *The Talmud of Jmmanuel* by Wild Flower Press. Semjase said that they enabled the *Talmud* to be found because the time for the truth had come.

This incredible book presents a very different interpretation of Jmmanuel/Jesus than that offered by the Bible. It says that he survived the crucifixion and then went on to live a long life, dying at an age of 110-115 in Srinagar, Kashmir, India. There he married at the age of 45 and had many children. The book explains that the person who betrayed Jmmanuel was not Judas Iscariot, his disciple, but was *Juda Ihariot,* the son of a Pharisee. Because his name was so similar to the famous disciple, it was easy for the enemies of Jmmanuel to falsely pin the blame on Judas. After the crucifixion Judas had gone into hiding and so could not defend himself against that false rumor. Judas accompanied Jmmanuel to India and eventually wrote down his true teachings. After Jmmanuel died around the age of 115, one of Jmmanuel's sons took Judas's manuscript to Jerusalem and buried it in the family tomb where Jmmanuel had been placed temporarily after the crucifixion.

The true teachings that Jmmanuel taught were the spiritual teachings that the Pleiadians had taught him. Basically, the *Talmud* says that we incarnate over and over in order to learn life's lessons and thereby perfect our spirit. And when we have perfected our spirit, we then merge with Creation and abide in the realm of all love and light. This ancient manuscript states that we are responsible for our own spiritual growth, that there is no savior other than the power of our own spirit, that our potential is unlimited, and it is most important that we develop ourselves spiritually and grow in wisdom and knowledge. Here, paraphrased in my own words, are some of the salient messages from *The Talmud of Jmmanuel:*

The greatest commandment is to achieve the wisdom of knowledge, for this will enable you to truly obey the laws of Creation. In other words, consider Creation alone as the supreme and ultimate power over all that exists.

You are immortal spirit, for you are a part of Creation, the Eternal Existence. It is your responsibility to save yourself by the power of your spirit—by the power of Creation within you. There is no other savior than your own spirit.

Let wisdom and knowledge be your friends and your source of happiness.

Life in the material plane is meant to be the process by which you perfect your spirit, lifetime after lifetime.

Humanity has not fallen from grace because it was never perfect in the first place.

Women should be treated fairly and should have the same equal rights as men do under the law.

The Sabbath is a day just like any other day. It is not Creational law that you shouldn't work on the Sabbath. That is a human-made law.

Body and spirit are one. Take care of your body so that your spirit has a healthy and adequate vehicle to experience life and learn what it needs to learn.

I, Jmmanuel, am not the son of God or the son of Creation. I am not the savior or the messiah. "God" is not Creation, but was the ancient Lyrian warlord Jehovan who once was ruler over Earth's people.

Truth and wisdom will elude those who follow the false teaching that proclaim me to be a god or a savior. I am a human being as you are, and only your own spirit can save you.

There is only oneness. The trinity of myself, Spirit, and Creation that will be professed in the future is a falsehood and is a corruption of my real teachings.

Mistakes made in life are a necessary part of your spiritual growth and are not "sins" that will be punished by a vengeful god or by Creation. You are to learn from your mistakes, thereby perfecting your spirit and gaining insight, knowledge, and wisdom.

Seek the truth, strive to grow spiritually, and learn to obey the laws of Creation and become one with Creation. This is the true purpose of life.

Study nature and you will learn the laws of Creation. Do this and you will grow in wisdom.

Perfect your powers of discrimination, insight, and wisdom. The greater your attunement to the laws of Creation, the greater shall be your peace.

Truth bestows real happiness.

Prayer is not necessary if your spirit is filled with wisdom. But if you do wish to pray, pray to the all-powerful spirit within you as follows: My almighty spirit, your name is sanctified. May your Kingdom and your power be born within me, both in my physical and spiritual life. Give me today your almighty power so that I can recognize my mistakes and learn from them and discover the truth. Lead me not into spiritual ignorance and confusion but redeem me from errors, for yours is the Kingdom within me and the power and knowledge in eternity.

Creation gives birth to new spirits which must perfect themselves through the reincarnational process. As the spirits evolve, Creation itself grows and becomes more perfect. Ultimately all spirits reunite with their source—Creation.

This book differs from the Bible in many ways. For example, instead of the rigid injunction to unconditionally and always love your enemies, the *Talmud* says: yes, love others, but do so with wisdom and common sense, and only when it is appropriate to do so. When someone slaps you on the cheek, you do not turn the other cheek to be also slapped. You rightly protect yourself by retreating or gently neutralizing the person's aggressive behavior. In other words, be a sane, rational, loving, spiritual being who can act appropriately in any circumstance, guided by wisdom, logic, rationality, and common sense.

It is this common-sense approach to life that so distinguishes the *Talmud of Jmmanuel* from the Bible. Many of the parables and stories in the *Talmud* are identical with those in the Bible. Often, though, they are completely opposite. One example: in the Bible it says to take no heed of tomorrow because God will take care of you. The *Talmud* says to take care of tomorrow, take care of your future needs, because that is the way of logic, love, wisdom, and common sense.

James Deardorff, a Bible scholar, has written an excellent book that attempts to authenticate *The Talmud of Jmmanuel*. His book, *Celestial Teachings—The Emergence of the True Teachings of Jmmanuel (Jesus)*, is published by Wild Flower Press as a companion book to *The Talmud of Jmmanuel*.

It is unfortunate that Billy Meier was the one to translate the *Talmud* since, by his own admission, 80% of the text now is in his "style" and only 20% is the original translation of Isa Rashid, the person who found the manuscript in Jerusalem. One wonders just how much Billy may have altered the original text.

Semjase told Billy many things about Jmmanuel. To paraphrase her once again in my own words:

Jmmanuel was only a human being, just like everyone else. He was, though, a very knowledgeable one and functioned as a teacher or prophet of spiritual knowledge and wisdom. He should not be idolized and adored. No creature should ever be idolized and adored. The truths he taught were not his truths but the truths of Creation, which Jmmanuel had to learn and recognize and accept. He simply taught and revealed what is natural law, what is eternally true. He was not the embodiment of his lessons and to regard him as such is a great error on the part of Earth humanity.

The truth of the Talmud should be learned without any glorification of Jmmanuel. The person of Jmmanuel is not important. The truth and the Creational laws he revealed are what is important. And these truths are eternally true. The truth remains for all time eternally the same.

The Talmud is the only record of Jmmanuel's teachings that was written during his lifetime. And it is the only book that contains the unfalsified lessons of the truth, knowledge, and wisdom of the spirit. It alone is able to expose the untruth of the New Testament of your Bible and to destroy in many people the madness of religion—or at least to greatly temper it.

The name "Christ" is a word meaning "the anointed one" and, strangely enough, was derived from an ancient satanic-type cult that had a practice of murdering virgins and babies and anointing themselves with the blood of their sacrificial victims. The Pleiadians suggested that we return to using the true name of that prophet—Jmmanuel. They also suggested we use the word "Creation" to describe the Great-All-Oneness, the incomparably magnificent force that has created all that exists. That we still refer to Creation as "Him" and "Creator" is simply a remnant of when we worshipped the Pleiadian warlord Jehovan as our "creator/god."

Billy Meier

Now we come to what is probably the most controversial aspect of Billy Meier and the Pleiadian material. The Pleiadians strongly intimated to Billy that he was the reincarnation of Jmmanuel (or that he was someone very closely linked to Jmmanuel). There are a number of places in the *Contact Notes* where Semjase all but declares that he was Jmmanuel. In any case, Billy apparently believes that he is the reincarnation of Jmmanuel. And in this lifetime Billy believes that he is simply continuing the mission he had started during that earlier lifetime. The Pleiadians told him that this time he didn't need to talk to large groups of people but instead to disseminate the eternal truths to mankind via books and other forms of mass communication. Both Billy and Semjase stress that it is of no importance who was Jmmanuel. What is important is the truth, not the messenger.

From all that I have learned about Billy Meier, I honestly don't know if he is, or is not, the reincarnation of Jmmanuel. It doesn't really matter to me, since I do believe that you are totally responsible for your own life and your own evolution. Neither Jmmanuel, nor Billy, nor anyone else is going to do your evolving for you. [For more on this subject, see pages 130-131.]

Each person has to find his or her own truth. Since there is no way of validating or invalidating most of the material in the *Contact Notes,* you just have to let your intuitive wisdom guide you in this matter. My advice is to follow your own heart and determine what is true for yourself.

Many of the ideas presented in this book can be hard to accept. I found some of the concepts presented in the *Contact Notes* to be unacceptable when I first encountered them. For example, because I looked upon androids as humans being exploited by the Pleiadians, it took me many years to come to terms with the idea that they used androids to do their menial labor. Eventually I came to understand that the androids were machines, not humans, and so were not slave laborers. They had partially organic bodies and minds and partially machine bodies but they had no soul or spirit and therefore were never "humans." Such concepts as androids, hyperspace, time travel, etc. are so far beyond our level that to begin to understand, or to even accept them, can take a long, long time. And much mental struggle.

Part II

Semjase Speaks

The Truth According to the Pleiadians

In three of the earliest contacts in 1975 between the Pleiadians and Billy Meier, the universal principles of spirituality were presented in great detail by Semjase. During those talks she told Billy about the secrets of life and death, man and God, religion and spirituality, and the real nature of our eternal spirit.

CHAPTER SIX

NINTH CONTACT
March 21, 1975

In some of the earliest contacts Semjase told Billy that they wanted to teach him about Pleiadian spirituality because that was of paramount importance for humanity. During three of those contacts in 1975, Semjase talked at great length regarding the truth about life, the universe, religions, spirit, and Creation. Here, paraphrased in my own words, is what she said during the ninth contact with Billy. The paragraphs are in the same order as Semjase originally spoke them.

Each human being is a vessel for his or her spirit. This spirit never dies and never sleeps. Even in deepest sleep, one's spirit is awake and is recording all thoughts and feelings and experiences. Your spirit can inform you if your thoughts are right or wrong if you take the time to observe yourself as you truly are and you accept the intuitive guidance of your spirit.

This spirit in each person is the carrier of the domain of Creation. It is that domain of Truth, Knowledge, Wisdom, Spirit, and Existence for which each person longs. For that is what never perishes and lasts for eternity. Heaven and Earth will disappear, but the Creational Domain of Truth, Knowledge, Wisdom and Spirit will never change or perish.

The realm of the spirit is the realm of perfection, harmony, peace, understanding, knowledge, wisdom, truth, beauty, love, recognition of one's real being, and all the things that last forever. Together, these form the spiritual kingdom. All this exists in Creation. All this is present as existence itself, as ability of all abilities, as the melody of all melodies, as wonder of all wonders, as the highest creational principle.

In dreams, humans can create worlds just as in reality, Creation creates worlds. This ability comes from man's consciousness, which is of Creation. All marvels exist within oneself. In your very own self is the heavenly kingdom, this wondrous Domain of Creation. This is the source of that ancient truth that everything that exists in the universe also exists in the human being. Thus the human is the microcosm in the macrocosm.

The inner realm within oneself is endless. This realm is spirit and it is a copy of the Creation. It is transcendent of all dimensions while at the same time containing all dimensions. It is the wonder of all wonders and is the source of all power. Wonder means the expression of spiritual power in perfection.

When you are happy, this experience comes from within, not from without. Joy is a self-created state and comes from spiritual balance. By spiritual effort one creates happiness and good fortune, for such comes from one's inner being. Outer good fortune in the world is not the cause of happiness but is instead the outward expression of the joyous fruits of spiritual unfoldment. The realm of spirit is one of infinite bliss and infinite power.

Spirit is forever young and it never grows old. The body may age, problems and grief may beset one, but all these outer conditions and experiences of the world pass away. What remains is the existence of spirit, which is Truth, Knowledge, Wisdom, and Reality. What is important in life is to work at developing one's spirit because only thus will you become free. When you realize that you are spirit you never again will be troubled by old age, sorrows, problems, and the innumerable vicissitudes of the world.

Wisdom is all-powerful. Wisdom is light. And wherever there is light, darkness and ignorance disappear. The light of wisdom overcomes all darkness. Wisdom is a sign of the existence of spirit and contains within itself the qualities of truth, beauty, harmony, knowledge, peace, and good fortune.

Wisdom is also the mark of anyone who has recognized the existence of his spirit and is diligently applying himself to be aligned with Creational law. The use of spiritual power is wisdom.

Just as sunlight and the sun are two, yet one, so are wisdom and spirit two, yet essentially one. Sunlight is produced by the sun just as the all-powerful Creation produces everything that exists. And all is governed by creational laws. This great Unity creates the forces that in truth, knowledge, and wisdom give witness to the peace of Eternity.

There is only one existence that governs all that exists throughout the universe. There is only one Creation, only one truth, one knowledge, one wisdom, that alone exists for all time. The eternal truth is unchanging, now and forever.

When religion claims to be the voice of Creation, as so many earthly religions do, then wisdom is negated. Spiritual force is all-powerful, but earthly religious heresies are just a sign of human weakness. The unreal teachings of earthly religions lead humans to search elsewhere for power, liberty, joy, and light— everywhere but where they can truly be found.

Wisdom is the mark of Creation within one. One's spirit is Creation within the human being. You should enlarge your wisdom, for by doing so you will come to know Creation. Seek the truth, and the power of your wisdom will grow. The truth frees you from all bondage and limitations and brings unlimited knowledge and wisdom. This wisdom enables you to know the laws of Creation.

One who is filled with love is also rich in wisdom, and one who is rich in wisdom is also full of love. Earthhumans deceive themselves for they know not love. They think that feelings of possessive desire are love.

You become a real human being when you realize the truth, the knowledge, and the wisdom even if you do not use the word "Creation." Love in its best form is wisdom. So the human being always discovers that understanding and enlightenment are also wisdom and love; and where love rules, there also rules wisdom.

Love and wisdom belong together because Creational laws are at the same time love and wisdom. Where Creation is, there is love and understanding. Where there is love and understanding, there is wisdom and knowledge.

It is through love and wisdom that the human being learns to know Creation. First know the truth and thereby achieve freedom and imperishable, eternal, peace. By wisdom and love the human being becomes master of all creation, for wisdom and love are the liberating wings of Creation within oneself. These two wings increase the desire to follow the natural creational laws, because spirit and Creation are one thing.

You cannot contain love in words because love, like bliss, is a state of being. Love is eternal and nothing can change love into another thing.

The spiritual path is one of gaining understanding of truth, knowledge, wisdom, and love.

Spirituality is meant to help spread truth, knowledge, wisdom, and love. If it doesn't, then it is not true spirituality but is an enslaving force of ignorance such as the cultish earthly religions. When spiritual teachings help strengthen the spirit, then such teachings are a mighty instrument of creational order. Such a spirituality spreads light and love and peace and teaches the eternal wisdom and truth that overcomes death.

The peace that is the peace of infinite existence is beyond man's understanding. To experience such peace is the true key for real understanding and wisdom. [Author: which is why the Pleiadians give such an experience to their people by taking them into hyperspace where they are immersed in the realm of eternal light, peace, and love.]

Within the kingdom of spirit are hidden wonders beyond wonders. The visible universe is only a small speck in this marvelous infinite spiritual existence of the Creation. And there are billions of universes in Creation. What the physical eye can see is only the tiniest fraction of the infinity. What is not visible is immeasurable, inconceivable, and unimaginable for our limited mind. This whole universe we see is just one of many. There are universes in universes, universes opposite universes, universes above and below universes, and universes outside the universes in this glorious, mighty, all-creating spiritual intelligence we call the Creation.

And a portion of this spiritual intelligence of Creation lives in each human as the spirit of that person. It is that spirit that enlivens each human. Each person is connected with Creation through his spirit.

Only the spiritually illumined know how great is the power of spirit and its joy, peace, liberty, wisdom, knowledge, and ability. The one who understands this truth and from that knowingness *creates knowledge, wisdom, and love is the one who is truly blessed. Such a one knows the answers to the last questions of science, philosophy, and the quandaries of daily human life.*

To become illumined like that you must seek the Truth and when found, generate from it knowledge, wisdom, and love, for only then will you be able to grow in truth, knowledge, wisdom, and love. This is real spiritual growth and this is what will free you from all human weaknesses.

When you remain constant in your thoughts of the Infinite, of the Creational-Spiritual Reality, then you are completely freed.

The spiritually wise abide by Creational law, they align themselves with Creation, and they strive towards helping the improvement of Creation itself. [Author: such as the helping by advanced races of more primitive races to evolve, i.e., the Pleiadians' telepathic guidance and influencing of present-day Earth culture.]

What a contrast with the materially minded human who concerns himself only with the objects of the world! Such people bring upon themselves great misfortune and are hindered and hampered in every direction.

Thus, it is essential for each person to analyze their life and face the truth and to choose the way of spiritual evolution. You need to look at your thoughts and see what they really consist of. Then align yourself with Creational-philosophical principles and realities and let the natural laws of Creation guide your life.

Strive toward a constant feeling that your spiritual being is one with Creation. By this method—that is, knowing that your essential spiritual existence is one with Creation—you can conquer the outer material world. This truth should govern your thoughts, feelings, and actions.

He who is one with spirit sees clearly, and with the full potential of Creation within can accomplish great things. Nothing in the universe can bind such an illumined spirit who sees one reality in all things and knows the eternal truth in the changeable, transitory forms.

What is a human being? Is it just a name and a body? If you take the name and body away, what is left? Spirit—the fundamental essence—remains. If you overlook this truth then you are as insecure and helpless as a leaf in the wind.

Billions of humans look up at the stars at night without any great comprehension of what they see as compared with the deep understanding of professional astronomers when they view the heavens. Just because you have eyes doesn't mean you can see. Similarly with normal and spiritual beings. The latter, living from deep knowledge of Creational laws, recognize, see, and understand that all that is around them, all forms of life, all objects, all thoughts and actions, all workings of nature, and all the myriad circumstances and events in life are just the manifestation of the One Creation.

The normal materialistic human, led astray by unreal dogma and cultish religion, is not able to see, or hear, or understand one bit of truth. He is blind and spiritually ignorant.

But the one who follows Creational law becomes fearless and full of bliss. He becomes resolute, unconquerable, and his wisdom and love are perfected and made constant. He experiences an immeasurable tranquillity, unlike the restless instability of the fickle and doubting religious-minded person.

The mind of a truly spiritual person doesn't indulge in either excessively negative or excessively positive thinking. Such a balanced mind, grounded in the deep and wise understanding of Creation and the need for service to Creation, is of paramount importance for spiritual development.

True spirituality, its love and delight, its wisdom and knowledge, is more real than all that exists in the material world. One's spirit is the innermost self of each human and is always great and constructive. The outer self is full of limitations because it is not the real self but is just the outer structure, just a limited human body, a source of pain and struggle, limited in its understanding, will, readiness for sacrifice, freedom, love, and good fortune.

If you observe only the outer material reality of a person, you miss the essential truth of the real person. Only by viewing with the understanding of spiritual insight do you see that the all-knowing consciousness within one person is the same as within every other person. Then you can love others as you love yourself. For you then see others as being, in essence, identical with yourself. Then you no longer see a man, or a woman, or a child, but instead you see that each one is really just Creation wanting to reveal itself through everyone. We each are vessels for a Creational spirit. Know this and see the Creation in all.

If you seek and accept the truth, you can deliver yourself from all ignorance. You can lose everything except your Creational consciousness. You can be deprived of all your possessions and be exiled from your homeland, but you can never be exiled from your inner spiritual kingdom.

So you should ever be conscious of Creation, without which you could not take one breath, could not think one thought, could not see, hear, or experience anything. Thus the wise say that Creation is closer to you than your own breath.

You cannot escape your spiritual destiny of realizing Creational consciousness because that is the life of your life and is your true identity. The spirit can exist without your eyes, ears, arms, legs, or even your mind. It is by the power of Creational force that your spirit is able to continue on.

Creation is of absolute importance and is the force behind the spiritual evolution of human beings. Creation gives rise to one's spirit, which is omniscient, omnipresent, and omnipotent. Thus, behind one's spirit is infinite bliss, infinite beauty, and infinite love.

Each time one thinks the word "Creation" or "spirit," one is raised higher and is blessed. Your heart and mind consequently change for the better.

The more light your spiritual intelligence gains, the more powerful becomes your character and the more blessed is your life. You can see far into the future and far into the past, and unlimited knowledge is yours. For within you is the whole spiritual empire, and he whose inner eye is open can see all.

Each person has the whole kingdom of the spirit within, but it is hidden by one's ignorance, imperfections, and faults until one sees and accepts the Truth. By correcting all your faults and negative habits you will become balanced and poised. You will gain spiritual experience by your seeking, finding, and understanding the Truth. This will lead to universal love and wisdom and the realization that the Creation is present in all.

In the spiritual kingdom, the human being is one with everything in the universe. He is one with truth, wisdom, and love.

Even though you seem to be separate beings isolated by space, time, and different bodies, you and your fellow humans are, in truth, one.

When you unite love and wisdom, knowledge and truth, then your heart and mind are blessed with the experience of oneness—the knowingness of Creation—the bliss of universal joy, power, and perfection.

Unfortunately, humans are presently ignorant of Creation and are misled by the false teachings of spirit-enslaving religion. Obeying society's laws in no way corresponds with knowing and obeying Creational law. With their false doctrines, earthly religions imprison people in spiritual ignorance and spiritual slavery. They prevent one from finding one's source—the spirit and the Creation.

One's daily life is divine, for the whole domain of daily worldly life is of Creation. [Author: There is no split between the worldly and the spiritual.] *One is infinite, eternal, and omnipresent. You are spirit, and spirit is Creation. You are all and all are you, because Creation is in everything and it is the spirit which enlivens everything. Thus the all is just one.*

How can you experience the oneness with the All when you are ignorant of your spiritual identity, when you misidentify yourself as being just a physical body? But if you seek the Truth and look within for your spiritual reality, for that spark of Creation within yourself, then you will experience the whole world dissolving into a spiritual oneness. Everywhere rules this one single Creational-Spiritual principle.

You focus on your body obsessively and you neglect your spirit. If you experience pain, then you become angry and sink into self-pity, lash out at others, and contemplate suicide. You

surround your body with vanity, fear, sorrows, pride, and problems. You relate everything to your body. You extend your bodily
identification out onto your physical possessions. You even get
angry when another accidentally touches your body.

When you turn to spirituality and understand the truth, then
you will identify with all the creatures of the world, with all the
creatures of the entire universe. You will see yourself as the All,
because you are then full of Creational-Spiritual truth, knowledge, love, and understanding. You know that the All comes from
the truth. Hence you identify with all and everything eternally.

You see yourself as your neighbor—spiritually, mentally, and
physically. With such a universal identity, of course, you will
treat your neighbor like yourself. Greed and hate can't exist in
you because you no longer see yourself as separate from others.
You become one with the Being in all.

Others may claim something as their exclusive property, but
the spiritually-minded person identifies himself only with the truth
in anything—never losing sight of the essential oneness—and thus
is not disturbed from the peace of his spiritual centeredness.

When you identify with the truth, you become completely freed
from all fear. All of Creation protects and serves the spiritually
attuned. If enemies attack you, that just strengthens you spiritually. Everything that happens to you in your life serves your
spiritual growth and furthers your understanding of the truth.

Those who wish to harm the spiritually-minded person by
criticism, lies, and ridicule, only injure themselves and demon-
strate their spiritual foolishness and ignorance. From such
attacks the spiritual person learns and grows and becomes
stronger in spirit. This is the truth.

The average human being, led astray by false earthly religions, is full of fanciful imaginings, wrong ideas, heresies, and delusions. To free yourself of such limiting ignorance, you must face the truth and surrender to true Creational spirituality.

All human delusion can be remedied by this truth: I am part of Creation, and that part of Creation is spirit, which is what gives me life.

Only spirit, only the force, truth and reality of Creation/Spirit, is real. Know this and you will rise to the heights.

The Truth is eternally valid. Never, and under no circumstance, will Truth need correcting. Truth does not need to be changed to adapt to a new time. Truth is constant for all times. Even if told in new words, the Truth will sound the same. Truth is the rock upon which to build your house for all time and places. The Truth existed before life and will exist afterwards.

What is short-lived is delusion. Creation and Truth are eternally the same, equal now and forever. They are unaffected by changing names and forms, for Creation and the Truth are nameless and formless.

Cling fast therefore to the Creational, for the Creational alone is eternally true. Truth is imperishable, just as Creation itself. Truth is perfect, eternal, and worthy of all one's efforts to attain it. When attained, the Truth forever frees you from falling into delusion. Then you hold fast to the Truth and become imperturbable and even-minded, filled with joy, knowledge, love, strength, and wisdom in all matters.

The Creational is infinite Wisdom, Truth, and is perfect. Look to the creational Wisdom within you and seek the light of your own spirit. A spiritual being knows that Creation is ever-present, and this Truth fills him with eternal joy. The infinite, indescribably powerful Creation surrounds him wherever he goes. He knows that he cannot even move his hand without touching the Creational because it is present in everything, in all time, in all space.

The Creational is full of infinite peace, understanding, and perfect perfection. It is the source of the wonders of highest spiritual consciousness—existing everywhere, both inside and outside of oneself. The spiritual life is one of unbounded bliss.

You hasten your spiritual evolution when you look at everything as being of Creation. Realizing anything, you realize the Creational. Behind all forms, as well as appearing as the form, stands Creation.

Therefore, you needn't run elsewhere to seek spiritual development, but instead, find it exactly where you are. For that is the best place to gain experience and understanding. You help your spirit develop and evolve by your thoughts and actions. Your spirit is within yourself, not somewhere else.

Understanding this, your attitude then becomes spiritual and you treat as holy the very earth beneath your feet. The spiritual human being looks not to the future to experience the Creational and his living spirit but to the present, here and now. To him, all time is now.

The realization of the Truth is not a physical thing. Seeking the Truth, man realizes more and more that what he seeks is his own ever-present spirit. To hasten his progress, he is willing to let anything into his consciousness. He listens intensely and deeply to all that he hears, and with a discerning mind he absorbs the truth. Each and every circumstance of this life he views as an opportunity given to him by Creation in order to help his spiritual growth. By such an understanding, man progresses spiritually.

Most people at present are very limited in their understanding and don't realize that the infinite Creation abides within as unlimited potential for spiritual growth. To awaken to oneness with Creation necessitates a mind that is capable of reason and logic and is free from false teachings.

This is the goal of life: to awaken the infinite within and have it guide your life. This constitutes real spiritual improvement.

Those who are rich in spirit become the instrument through which Creation expresses the spiritual kingdom. They bring Heaven upon the Earth. The rich in spirit are unfettered, ego-free, and are ever aware of Creation. Humans now ignore the importance of the spiritual while at the same time they overemphasize the material. Soon, though, your sciences will discover that every creature has a spark of Creation itself within its being and it is that Creational spark that propels its evolution.

Creation itself and the spirit within are alone true freedom, true perfection, true understanding, power, love, truth, and wisdom. In their essence they are the Creational itself.

To achieve anything of real importance in life you must turn to true spirituality, for that is the unlimited and unlimitable. Everything that is limited and limitable carries with it unreality and problems. Such may appear attractive initially, but eventually the limited gives rise to sorrow and illusion.

Misfortune and grief come to those who worship the finite rather than the infinite. The finite always brings only problems and difficulties. All that is finite passes away, so grieve not for what is transitory.

All things finite are subject to change. One day you may love something, and the next day you hate it. What passes away will pass away, and what is eternal will forever remain.

When your wisdom, truth, and spiritual knowledge increase—when universal love guides your life—when your life is a blessing for yourself and for others—then know that your understanding of the Truth has come to fruition. Then you will know that you and Creation are one, now and forever.

Strive towards spiritual light and spiritual love, and the door to Creation will be opened for you. When you love the Truth, then you love what is perfect and wonderful, for the Truth embodies the spiritual kingdom itself and is also the way to the kingdom of wisdom.

Then you are conscious of Creation here and now, in everything, everywhere. Even in the depths of space you are comforted by knowing that Creation is there with you.

The spiritually-minded person is consciously connected to Creation and can obtain answers to anything, anywhere, anytime. He strives continuously to live a spiritual life of conscious awareness of oneness with the all-powerful Creation.

CHAPTER SEVEN

ELEVENTH CONTACT
April 15, 1975

During the eleventh contact, Semjase again talked at length about what is true spirituality. To paraphrase her in my own words:

The true seeker of spirituality is a noble artist of precious spirit, kind character, and is full of love, knowledge, and wisdom. He is high-minded and is receptive to truth, beauty, balance, and spiritual progress. His perspective is vast. His life is orderly and his mind is clear and generous.

Beauty is expressed in his unpretentious life that is full of spiritual dignity. His inner peace has a beauty that no artist could capture in a painting nor any poet could describe with words. Not even the most beautiful harmonious music could express his spiritual tranquillity that is so powerfully attractive.

He is self-assured, and confident that he could accomplish any goal. His wisdom is like a light that penetrates the most hidden darkness. It is not like the light of day which fades into nothingness in the darkness of night. Neither is it like the mind of great human thinkers whose mental powers can wane with old age. His presence exudes the fragrance of eternity and it never fades, unlike the rose which perfumes the air for only a short time after blossoming.

It is the spirit which is the measure of all things; never is the human being the measure. The human being is made up of numerous layers that hide his actual personality from others. He may identify himself as his physical body and seek to satisfy the demands of the body. Or he may identify with his mind, or he may identify with his real self—his innermost spirit which witnesses the body and mind. But the human being cannot create himself.

The physical body and all that is associated with it, appropriate though they may be in the physical plane of existence, cannot forever suppress the spiritual from emerging. And if physicality does for a while overshadow the spiritual, it is very confusing to one's spirit.

In the body-identified human being, the material intellect rules his life, and spiritual development proceeds very slowly. The spiritual intellect needs to be developed consciously, because one doesn't proceed from material intellect to spiritual intellect development automatically. For the mind just goes in circles like a dog chasing its tail.

The materialistic mind is superficial and is unable to penetrate to the core of reality. Only with the spiritual intellect can you merge with something and thereby truly know it for what it is.

If you really want to know someone you must be able to identify with them and to spiritually merge into oneness with them. Also, if you want to fully comprehend a matter, you need to identify with it and be one with it.

The material intellect only observes things with the physical senses and from objective sensory data. And from that it derives its conclusions. But that approach ignores the more penetrating and ultimately more satisfying impressions one can glean by using one's spiritual intellect.

Through all time, through all universes, spiritual thinkers have occupied themselves with the truth that the real self is not the physical body or mind but is the immortal spirit within oneself. This spirit is the invincible light that never gets extinguished.

The body is always changing; one's thoughts are always vacillating; but the essential being is steady and constant and is able to handle everything. It is the fundamental origin of the feeling "I am"—of self-identity, remaining as a constant throughout all the changes in life. It remains the same while all else around it changes.

The limited human personality is only partially conscious, and even in that partialness it is only intermittently conscious.

When the human being dies, only the body dies. The spirit, the knower within, does not die for it is a part of Creation and is eternal. Nothing objective can touch the knowing, subjective self. This eternal self, which is the life of one's life, cannot be seen with physical eyes because it is of purely spiritual form and nature. One who knows himself spiritually does not demand physical evidence of spirit because his spirit is, in and of itself, its own validation. Only those who live in spiritual poverty demand evidence to prove the existence of spirit. Being so spiritually primitive, they are not able to understand the existence of spirit from perceiving the spiritual facts.

Spirit itself is the fundamental substratum of all knowing. Spirit itself gives life to each organ and to each ability. It does this to maintain life and to enable each creature to evolve.

The confused, spiritually ignorant human being can easily misidentify himself with the objective physical and mental self. When he drops this misidentification, even though he still lives in a physical body, he reaches the true destination of his life.

Spirit is simple, easy, uncomplicated, and is of the nature of reality, understanding, knowledge, wisdom, love, and freedom. Man is not just a biological phenomenon.

Inside each person is a spiritual-Creational self that has infinite potential. Knowing this inner self of man, you know Creation. Know yourself not just as a body and mind, but also as a psychic-spiritual being.

All that has ever happened to you, all that you have enjoyed, experienced, read, or learned, lies hidden in your subconsciousness. Why don't you master your mind and through concentration, access all of your knowledge and ability?

Deep within you is the desire to know all that is hidden in your subconscious mind. Just see the truth of this and that acknowledgment will set you on the path to great wisdom.

Put aside your foolishness and see that the material intellect does not express the truth of who you are, unless the material intellect is functioning in cooperation with the spiritual intellect.

When you do understand that your spirit is who you truly are, the great storehouse of wisdom and knowledge from all your previous incarnations will be available to you.

Knowledge, power, wisdom, liberty, and love are your spiritual inheritance from Creation, and it is all yours by right of your simply having been born a human being.

Man is the center of thought, power, force, and influence onto all and everything. Man has a body, but his body is not him. It is only a vehicle, an instrument, a servant of his spirit. The body houses man's spirit. It does not imprison his spirit. It is the temple of the spirit—of the shining inner self that is of Creation.

This spirit within the body castle is the real driving force of man. Know that it is spirit that breathes life into your body, not your body that breathes life into your spirit.

Through meditation—through contemplation—through the deepest submerging into the inner silence of the spiritual self—will you learn to know your spirit.

Meditation does not mean the fanciful imagining that religiously deluded people believe meditation to be. Real meditation in its spiritual form necessitates increased understanding of your self, of your real being. It demands the seeing that all is one and that the whole is forever balanced.

It is only because you are already, in your innermost essence, a manifestation of Creation that you are able to unite with the infinity. To contemplate and deliberate about these matters regarding the essential existence of the Creational gives rise to real wisdom and positive knowledge.

Look at truth directly and the false will fall away. Realize the truth and all questions will be answered. Do not expect to find eternal happiness on Earth, for only the spiritual realm can give you lasting satisfaction.

Life in the material plane is a means to spiritual life—it is not the end or ultimate goal. Material life is only a stage upon which you can have a myriad of experiences, and its value lies in its preparing you for spiritual life.

Beware of letting the material realm obscure your higher vision of spirit. Don't value things just by their materialistic value. The true value of a life depends on how high you rise spiritually to a greater attunement with the Creational.

Human relationships are justified only insofar as they comply with the eternal laws of the spiritual nature. The evolvement of mankind, spiritually and socially, is only possible if you turn to true spirituality—to the essential core of reality.

The essential core of Truth does not belong to any one person because it is the Truth that has given life to all that exists. That Truth is the oneness within that spiritually unites each person with the all. Realization of that oneness is the culmination of life, the achievement of the ultimate goal. In that oneness lies the ethical base for social and domestic relations.

Society is the collective whole, whose destiny is to penetrate all veils until the ultimate goal of immortal existence is reached by uniting in oneness with Creation itself.

Human life is meant to be lived not in spiritual darkness and ignorance, but in spiritual illumination. This enables one to be less and less bound by the material plane and the material intellect, and more and more to love and be attached to the spiritual.

To live so in harmony with the Creation, with spirit that knows no limits, gives rise to altruistic love whereby you love all that exists as yourself, for your self is the all.

When a family, society, or a nation sees itself as separate beings, then that attitude precludes success. Only with an attitude that all are connected, that all are of the One, can a family, society, or a nation achieve real success. Only by living from that truth of essential oneness can a human live in harmony with universal events.

Life is meant to teach spiritual lessons to your spirit. All of Creation is governed by Creational law. Creation dictates that families as well as countries obey natural, Creational law.

Just as Creation itself is perfect and harmonious, so needs to be each human being, for each one lives only because of the existence of Creation. Humans live and exist in the Creational Existence.

In the absence of true spirituality to guide his life, the human being goes astray and creates inharmony and suffering and crises in his personal life and all concerning him.

Modern man has been unsuccessful in his search for peace and freedom because he lacks real knowledge and truth of a rational, reasonable way of life that is capable of giving him inner balance and peace.

Man has instead turned to unnatural ideologies and to dangerous, harmful, and transitory religious philosophies that lead him into greater spiritual poverty and prevent him from attaining the real life.

Natural human reason rebels against such unreal religious dogmas, so prevalent on Earth at the moment. Earth's religions, with their great confusion and deluded claims, lessen the inner, spiritual force within humans. This inner force maintains the spirit of the human and nurtures his striving for greater spiritual heights and deeper states of inner peace, as well as for balance in his life in regard to outer achievements and circumstances.

Modern philosophers have tried to extract the best from religions and combine that with modern thinking to create a philosophy of life more suited for present-day mankind. But these philosophers don't realize that in their ignorance, all they have done is increase religious delusion. They themselves are imprisoned in unreal religions and so all that they can do is express their superstitious delusion and their spiritual poverty. Thus, they have utterly failed to help humanity.

Now, however, humanity has been given the Truth and so can easily solve previously intractable problems. Man can build a new philosophy and value system based upon these teachings of true spirituality. In the future, mankind can build this new philosophy and create a life of spiritual freedom based on the best of the cultural and spiritual inheritance of Earth and on the eternal Spiritual Truth.

Man will achieve this wonderful life of spiritual freedom when he frees himself from all religions and their delusional fancies and then finally turns to the spiritual and Creational laws. Religion throws man back into darkness. Only the Truth can enable man to progress and evolve.

CHAPTER EIGHT

EIGHTEENTH CONTACT
May 15, 1975

During the eighteenth contact, Semjase presented her third in-depth presentation of what constitutes true spirituality. Here, again in my own words, is a paraphrase of what she told Billy Meier:

When hearing the word "Creation" you should be affected in the same way as when hearing about something exquisitely beautiful and good. And if you are not so affected, then you haven't realized the glorious wonder that is the Creation.

Reflect upon the nature of Creation and that will enable all the love and joy within your heart to rise up and fill you with bliss. Just consider the extraordinary and wonderful descriptions often used in relation to the Creation: almighty, omnipresent, and omniscient.

The common man, the atheist, the egoist, the materialist, and the agnostic are not moved by the word "Creation." Why? Because they have no idea what the word really refers to. Billions of religiously deluded humans fail to comprehend what the word "Creation" means. They incorrectly use the term "God" as if that were an appropriate word for Creation. [Author: "God" is the old Earth term for a king of wisdom or IHWH/Ishwish, which was a Lyrian warlord ruling over ancient Earth thousands of years ago. Jehovan was the first Lyrian warlord to call himself "God" and pretend to be the creator of the primitive Earthhumans.]

You need to learn as much as possible about the real nature of Creation so that when you hear that word it evokes all your heart's love. Creation is infinite beauty, a beauty beyond all beauty. Creation is all goodness. Creation is wisdom, knowledge, ability, truth, and the goal above all goals.

The discerning human can trace the source of every joy and delight of his life back to the infinite bliss of Creation. When he sees beauty in a flower, an animal, or a human, or anything, he sees that the beauty comes from Creation itself.

And whenever he comprehends anything profoundly, he knows that the understanding comes from the infinite wisdom of Creation.

All life, even the tiniest microbe, comes from the Eternal Creation. Wise is he who deepens his love and understanding of Creation and who feels the presence of Creation in every moment of his daily life.

Within each and every human being is a piece of Creation itself. If this concept can just once penetrate you, then in the experiencing of that truth you will be forever freed from all fear and doubt.

Knowing that Creation is omniscient and all-powerful, you have a feeling of peace and security within that protects you from silly fears and apprehensions.

Repeated reflection upon the nature of Creation—its eternal-ness, omnipresence, truth, and wisdom—will align your heart and mind with the magnificence that is the Creation. Turn your mind towards Creation—and your life will be filled with bliss and your being will be full of power. Then your mind will be like a beacon of light.

The spiritual human being always sees himself as spirit rather than as a physical body. This feeling is supreme and constant and rules his life. Because of this, he is full of peace, strength, joy, knowledge, wisdom, and hope.

Only the spiritually minded man is empowered by the dynamic force of Creation It is futile for man to try to find peace, power, and happiness solely through the use of his material intellect.

The spiritual human is quite dynamic in everything he does. He incessantly endeavors to achieve his goals as quickly as possible. As long as he is alive, he strives with all of his being to grow spiritually. No matter what happens to him, he never gives up on his quest for union with the Creation. He may encounter great obstacles in life and he may lose all desire for material necessities, but he never loses his desire for Creation, because he knows that the Creation embodies his true self.

Only those who strive with all their being achieve their highest spiritual goals. They know that truth, knowledge, logic, wisdom, and love don't come to a person without spiritual effort.

They know that first they have to learn the spiritual-intellectual way of thinking. They understand that only by learning this Creational way of thinking will they have their first successes in their spiritual development. And when such does happen, then their understanding and their spiritual power advance in leaps and bounds. Truth becomes self-evident to such a spiritually awakened one.

Seeking, searching, exploring, developing, growing, he eventually finds the formless, eternal infinity. He lets nothing divert him from his spiritual path. He knows that all time is now, that the future is here, in the present. He understands that he must do all that he needs to do here and now if he is to reach the highest spiritual consciousness.

Because the future is fully present in the here and now, as present as the present is, he has no fear of the future. Such fear of the future exists only in the material-intellectual way of thinking, never in the spiritual-intellectual way of thinking.

Thus, the spiritual man is able to control and solve the problems of tomorrow, today. Only by spiritual thinking can you be given such an advantage. True spiritual searching leads to real evolvement of the individual.

It is the Truth of Creation that empowers and frees man from the bondage of ignorance and false beliefs. Again and again man must see the truth that he exists in the ocean of Creational light, its wisdom, its knowledge, its logic, and its love.

It is the delight of the spiritual human to venerate Creation. He accepts the almighty will contained in Creational law and he makes these laws his own and applies them. He shows his devotion to Creational laws by learning and applying spiritual principles in his life.

The way to learn is to ceaselessly strive for higher spiritual understanding and to apply the resulting abilities that come from such understanding. Here is what constitutes real understanding and observance of Creational laws: patience and persistence in the development of higher understanding; realization and the use of cosmic and universal love; deepening of spiritual abilities and knowledge; and the elimination of egoism, excessive materialism, pride, greed, envy, etc.

The spiritual human strives to express the Creational outwardly from within himself as well as making it visible in himself and his life. To the common man, the successes of such an evolved soul seem miraculous.

Day after day, month after month, year after year, the spiritual human cries out for the Creational and by this he grows in knowledge, wisdom, love, logic, truth, and power, until at last he realizes the unity of himself and Creation. The feeling of this is more real than the feeling of his own body. When he relates to others and talks with them, he feels like it is only Creation that he is relating with. Creation is always first for him.

Because he has made the Creation foremost in his life, and he sees only Creation wherever he may be, he cannot be led astray by anything in the material realm.

Living spiritually as he does, worldly temptations cannot affect him because the truth-based existence in which he lives is incomparably more delightful than the most beautiful and enticing pleasures of the universe. Nor can great riches or threats of death from evil-minded creatures deter him from his spiritual path.

His inner riches of Creational attunement are inexhaustible and imperishable. Because of this he is absolutely fearless and indomitable in his personal power. Nothing can mislead him towards falseness because he abides in the Creation-inspired understanding of infinite truth. Nothing can alter his inner feeling of the Truth because he lives consciously in Creation, in a state of bliss and delight.

If a human being falls into habitual negative thinking patterns about himself or about Creation, nothing at all will succeed for him. Even if he is in quite favorable circumstances, a negative material-intellectual mind can influence his environment and bring misfortune and lack of peace to him.

But for a spiritual human, each and every thing will always be just the right circumstance for his inner growth and will be an opportunity to express his devotion to Creation.

Great indeed will be the human who develops and maintains his spirituality and high-mindedness, who keeps his mind on high and lofty thought of spirit. Those who live with constant awareness of the Creational inside are the only ones who can truly be called spiritual.

Those who are material-intellectual humans of greatness, religious saints, workers for peace, humanitarian helpers, first-aid medics and others who stay on the front lines in wars to give aid to the wounded, all these can be not Creational and can be utterly unimportant in terms of spirit.

In most such cases, these people are moved by thirst for adventure, pity and self-pity, and other wrong material-intellectual thoughts and are devoid of the deep understanding of the Creation within themselves.

Often they are misled by unreal religions, false love for their fellow man, and the desire to preach that false love of humanity along with godly doctrines of devotion to a deity.

[Author: the total context of the Pleiadian contacts with Billy make it plain that they are not against showing love and compassion toward one's fellow man, but they do stress that such actions are best when done in the context of true understanding of Creation and thus are done with the right motives. To serve man and to try to alleviate pain and suffering is good—but not if that means you ignore real spirituality and get lost in a worldly philosophy, focusing your life solely on humans and the material world. The

Pleiadians themselves were always extremely kind, courteous, compassionate, and loving to Billy and to each other.]

What are the differences between such humanitarian-worldly people and the truly spiritual human? The material-intellectual person is dominated by worldly concerns and is unable to maintain good feelings when they do arise.

The spiritual human, on the contrary, is able to seize hold of positive feelings and to enlarge them without limits. Low movements [Author: hate, greed, envy, fear, etc.] are unable to find a place to anchor in one whose wisdom and knowledge are so deep. He strives to always abide on a profound spiritual level. If he feels threatened by negative influences of any kind, he calls upon the Creation as his protector. He does this until the Creational being within himself has generated the necessary force to repel any negativity.

The material-bound human carries within himself feelings of low self-esteem along with grief, sorrows, problems, hopes, and other thoughts of a materially-minded nature. The spiritual human only carries that which is of a Creational or spiritual nature. He resolutely refuses to lower his vision from the Creational to that which is of a lowly level. He transforms any negative thought by the power of his spiritual wisdom. Thus, he turns everything into a positive nature and becomes a man of real power. He becomes a living temple of Creation.

His intelligence gets more spiritualized and he rises higher into spiritual consciousness. He sees to the heart of all matters and perceives the truth and power of the presence of Creation everywhere.

What can't be perceived by the everyday mind can be realized by his spiritual consciousness. He sees Creation and the working of

Creational laws in all things and in all life forms. And he devotes his life to learning about Creation and developing his spirit.

Worldly life is a transitory phenomena, but behind it exists the eternal truth—the spirit, the Creational presence, the reality of Creation itself. The Creational reality contains the entirety of wisdom and life-mastery abilities. This is the timeless truth that forever remains. This is the eternal love that is our destination.

Many people are afraid to face the reality of Creation. They want only to hide from their fear of death by believing in some god that promises them eternal security. The motive of "God" (the Lyrian despot, Jehovan) was to enslave humans, which he succeeded in doing by perpetuating religious heresies, generation after generation. [Author: For more information on Jehovan, please see Appendix No. 1.] *The imaginary delusions of religiously minded humans obstructs their spiritual thinking abilities.*

Only a few humans do not fear to live consciously in the reality of Creation. They know that that alone makes life really worth living.

CHAPTER NINE

SEVENTY-NINTH CONTACT
July 16, 1977

During the 79th contact, Semjase talked at length about spirituality for the last time. To paraphrase her in my own words:

Only the fog of ego prevents a human from having a truly spiritual life. This egotism happens when the ego overstresses the importance and worth of itself. Then the dark thunderclouds of doubts and insecurities and other unworthy concerns hang over the person. Egotism and materialism thus imprison the person. [Author: Awareness of your unique individuality is not negative egotism. Unbridled self-importance that harms others is the egotism that hinders spiritual growth].

The fear and sorrow of such a person are reasonless. Only when the sun of love rises above the horizon of your psyche will such thunderclouds disappear. Only then, by your awakening to true spirituality, will you find the inner security you desire.

Unfortunately, at the present time many people only awaken to spirituality when they die. But when they reincarnate, they may have to deal with the same type of circumstances as they did in their last life if they haven't raised their level of spirituality. Only if they persevered in growing spiritually during the last life will they reincarnate to a better life. It is you, by your own spiritual efforts, who determine your own fate. By the light of your spirit within, you see that it is the invisible power of spirit that governs life, not the outward visible things that control life.

Many Earthhumans greatly fear their own death. Also, they fear losing the love of close ones, or having a beloved one die. This is compounded by the ignorant belief that this life is the one and only life and you will never have another opportunity to live a life on the material plane.

Many people also mistakenly believe that life is a chaotic jungle where survival demands a kill-or-be-killed attitude. This is false, for Creation guides all life in order to have constant progressive evolution. Creation is orderly and is regulated by Creational laws of logic, love, and truth.

Within the great wheel of life and death, one experiences innumerable births and deaths. Birth and death complement each other and are two parts of one whole. Life does not strive against any one particular death but against death itself by evolving beyond the need for the physical life-death cycle. Life strives towards the ultimate goal—towards Creation, towards the Universal Consciousness.

The purpose of life in the physical plane is to conquer the ego self, the little I, and to enable the spirit to evolve by awakening to your higher spiritual self. Your higher self is the Creational I. While this is the most difficult of all things to achieve, it is the most beautiful, worthwhile, and highest goal of life.

Becoming the Creational self gives you the constant feeling of security of the eternal existence. You see that behind your little self is your Creational self. Your inner spirit is part of the spiritual energy of Creation itself and so by awakening to it you experience true freedom and you are released from all fear of death.

This is the most wonderful of all things—to realize that one's very own self, one's original I, is beyond anything one ever imagined, that one is of the infinite, the eternal, and a part of glorious Creation itself.

Whoever consciously unites himself to his spirit understands that death is but the other side of life and is no more to be feared than going to sleep at night. Just as you awaken from sleep to greet a new day, so do you awaken from death to greet a new life incarnation. Your spirit never dies. You are eternal.

Turn to the real task of earthly life—mastery of the physical plane of existence, mastery of the fine-matter plane of existence, and realization that both planes are simultaneously existing in the same place and at the same time but in different dimensions.

Pain and suffering are much more prevalent than joy and delight on Earth at present. But it need not be like this. Happiness and pleasure do not have to be balanced by pain and suffering as if they were two sides of a scale. You pay far too much attention to your suffering and much too little to your joy. You haven't yet learned how to distill the positive from your negative experiences. Realize the true destiny of man and that will enable you to transform your circumstances and will guide you from darkness to light.

You have millions and billions of years to grow and evolve so don't worry too much about your life and your destiny. But do seize this opportunity of guidance from us and reflect upon the truths that we have offered to you.

So ended the last of Semjase's major expositions on spirituality.

CHAPTER TEN

SELECTED SEMJASE PARAPHRASES
1975 to 1978

In truth, we Pleiadians are human beings just like Earth human beings, except that our wisdom and technical level are much higher.

Only Creation has power of life and death over each creature. Creational laws are eternal and irrefutable. Humans can recognize these laws by observing nature. These laws show humanity a way of life leading to spiritual greatness. Man is now being led astray through the following of Earth religions that are not based on truth. God is only a ruler, a governor, a human being. He is not Creation. Man deifies god and pretends god is Creation. And man deludes himself even more when he believes that Jmmanuel (Jesus Christ) is god's son and is the Creation itself. Religious leaders and other charlatans lie when they say we Pleiadians come on behalf of god to bring peace to humanity and to affirm Earth religions and to protect man and to create a new world order that deifies man's anthropomorphic "God."

Creation itself never commands, because Creation is all-powerful and is in no need of commands or religion. Religion is just a primitive ruse by some humans to suppress, control, and exploit other human beings. It is because of these primitive Earth religions that man is in such spiritual darkness.

We Pleiadians are not perfect and we are not supermen. We have to develop ourselves just as you do. Those who say we are perfect, that we are angels, or gods, are just fantasizing and projecting their own desire to put their responsibility to evolve onto another, to abdicate their own personal responsibility. That is why you have religions and gods—so you can put the responsibility all on god.

Some say that we are superhumans or that we are watchers of Earth and the controllers of the fate of humans. This is false, as we are just human beings. If we were the guardians of Earth-humans, we would regulate them openly. We perform a self-ordained mission which has nothing to do with supervising and regulating the fate of human beings on Earth. Even though we are thousands of years more advanced spiritually and technically than Earth society, we are not better or superior, we are just more evolved. And as Earth humanity evolves, it will discard the barbarism and religious fanaticism that presently hampers its progress. This putting aside of fanciful religious imaginings and instead cultivating real understanding will in no way lessen one's natural awe of life or the awe before Creation itself. On the contrary, as one's understanding and development increase, one's awe of Creation and life also increase.

We are not teachers or missionaries or wayshowers. But we do feel a duty to help developing life forms in the universe and to assist in maintaining order in the cosmos. We help young developing races emerge from ignorance by preparing them for the thought that they are not alone in the universe, that they are not the only thinking beings in existence. Also, by telepathy we influence races to develop certain timely inventions and certain thoughts and ideas. We don't openly contact Earth governments, because all the Earth governments are based on greed and power, not love and truth. All they would want from us would be our technology so they could conquer all the other countries and rule the world. And we don't openly show ourselves to the masses because they are bound by cultlike religions. People would venerate us as gods or become hysterical with fear if confronted with our presence on Earth. Therefore, it is most advisable to instead just contact one Earthhuman and let him slowly inform

humanity of our existence and our mission and to gradually
let humanity become prepared for contact with us.

Earthmen must grow spiritually, else they expand their race
into space and try to conquer other planets. They could meet
races who have the capacity to easily defeat Earth humanity and
enslave it, or completely annihilate it. If barbarous Earthhumans
try to export their greed and lust for power into outer space, then
more powerful races will respond with terrifyingly destructive
force and completely destroy humanity. There are many dangers
in the universe, mostly from power-thirsty creatures who lack love
in their hearts. Even if you remain in your own solar system,
someday you will have to deal with barbarous but technologically
advanced races. Only if all of Earth humanity unites into one
nation will you be able to fight off such evil intruders. Also,
there are races that are not advanced technologically, but who
are under the protection of more highly developed intelligences
whose technology has reached the last perfection of the material
plane. [Author: Earth seems to be in that position with
the Pleiadians.]

To grow spiritually, you must put aside belief and instead
really work at reasoning through things and building a foundation of real knowledge and understanding of reality. You must
put aside religion, for religion suppresses you and makes you
dependent upon an exterior authority. Then you can't be master
of your self. In all the universe there is no such thing as a good
religion. Religions create confusion and you get pulled between
the unreal and the real. You get lost in distortions and unreality.
Instead of seeking guidance through your cultlike Earth religions,
let truth and real spiritual understanding be your guide.

When a human being dies, his spirit goes to the fine-matter or
spirit-form realm where it lives as a spirit until it reincarnates
into a physical body in the material world once again. Simply

because one drops the physical body through death does not automatically confer greater wisdom upon a soul. The being has no more wisdom and spiritual knowledge after death than it did before death. Therefore, it is not advisable to try to confer with dead spirits in hopes that they will bestow great wisdom upon oneself. Better to increase your knowing by your own spiritual labors while alive. And while there are highly advanced spiritual forms that could give you great knowledge, these beings exist on such high planes that few Earthhumans could contact them. There are very few authentic mediums on Earth who have the ability to contact highly evolved spirits existing in the fine-matter realms.

Intelligence is not genetic but is caused by spiritual evolution. Spiritual knowings, wisdom, and intelligence are factors of the spirit and yet they do have a physical manifestation as the organic acids in the brain. It is possible to transplant the brain acids of an advanced being into a lesser developed being and to thus bestow great wisdom and intelligence into someone who lacks such wisdom and intelligence. When a Pleiadian woman falls in love with a less-developed man from some other star system, she can easily bring him up to her high level by the use of the advanced Pleiadian science.

In fact, whole races of beings can be brought up to a very high level of wisdom, knowledge, and intelligence by such means, without the need for each single individual having to go through the different evolutionary steps. Even an idiot, which is actually just a new spirit without much experience or wisdom, could be brought up to a high level of knowledge and life by this method.

Because intelligence is a product of the evolutionary level of the spirit, the offspring of low-intelligent humans could be geniuses and the children of highly intelligent parents could be idiots. This is because the incoming spirit could be more highly evolved or less evolved than the parents. It all depends on the spiritual level of the reincarnating spirit.

Deluded human Earthbeings consider themselves to be the only human beings in the universe and that they are the crown of Creation. We, as well as other star-traveling races, influence many good writers and inspire them to write of the truth, often first as science fiction. This prepares the human beings for the idea that they are not the only humans in the universe. We also influence scientists so they can make certain discoveries and help the race achieve a technical mastery appropriate for the age. As well, we try to hold back technical advances when appropriate to do so. Such is now the case on Earth, for humans are not spiritually evolved enough to handle wisely the powers they have unleashed.

In this, the Age of Aquarius, there are revolutionary changes happening, some good, some bad. The worst changes are the rise of cult-like religions that perniciously control humans. During the 184 years of transition time into the Age of Aquarius, from 1844 to 2028 A.D., many people who are religiously oriented will fall into fanatical delusion because of their Earthly religion. Murder, suicide, exploitation of all kind, and religious slavery due to false beliefs become predominant in the world. False prophets and evangelists offering salvation publicly promote themselves and frantically search for victims to exploit. All this is happening at the same time that science is rapidly developing, the crime rate is rising, and wars are rampant. Not until February 3, 2028 will the Golden Epoch finally be established. On February 3, 1937 the Earth reached the end of the Piscean Age. It was at 11:20 a.m. that day that Eduard Meier was born, destined to be the prophet of Truth for the new age.

The origin of these epochs is the sun's circling around a huge central sun every 25,860 years. Earth scientists call this the "progression of the equinoxes" and they divide it into 12 different epochs named after your zodiac. The Earth has already entered into the outer border of the central sun. These "golden radiations" that the Earth is now receiving are the strongest and most transformative radiations in the universe. It is because they cause the greatest evolution that this Aquarian Age is also called the Golden Age, the New Age, or the Revolutionary Age.

The whole solar system and all its creatures are influenced by this new age. All human laws that are not consistent with Creational law will be fashioned anew so that they are aligned with Creation. Over many centuries mankind will gradually discard unreason and will arrange everything according to creational-natural laws. This is a sublime and exciting and important age for it will influence all later ages. During this time, humans will find a natural spiritual direction. Many, though, will die still in delusion from their religion. Fortunate will be those who flee the heresies of religion and dedicate themselves to the truth, the knowledge, and the wisdom of the spirit.

At the high point of the Aquarian Age, all that is spirit-obstructing and spirit-enslaving will be eradicated. Only those who are spiritually-minded will remain. Those with true spiritual knowledge and abilities will dominate the world and all those without the inclination to attune themselves to higher spheres of the spiritual and to walk in harmony with others will be eliminated by the natural forces of life. A true harmony and balance will be created on Earth.

The way-preparers of this revolutionary time are those who announce the truth of knowledge and spiritual wisdom and who proclaim that religion does not lead to spiritual development but to stagnation and regression. Because their message is a direct challenge to the existing order and to the power of the religions that dominate the world, they will be accused of deceit and quackery. But the revelations and spiritual teachings of truth *that these way-preparers present to humanity are of the utmost importance and should be spread by all means. That is our desire.*

We allow you to take photographs of our beamships to help people awaken to the truth of our existence. But we don't allow everyone to actually see our beamships because the cognition of the reality of our existence must be founded upon spiritual hard work that creates knowledge, understanding, and true reasoning. We will not coerce humans to convince them that we exist.

Religious imaginings hamper progress in every direction and can even stifle people in the bud of their spiritual awakening. True progress only happens when religious fancies are put aside and you search for truth where it is really hidden.

Barbarism will drop away as humanity gains the necessary spiritual understanding.

We present the basic Creational laws and truths to humanity to help them evolve, but we don't show ourselves to the masses because then we would be seen as teachers, and people would not do the hard spiritual work that they must do by their own efforts. You must think for yourself and labor spiritually with your own mind to elaborate the truth and gain wisdom and knowledge. Only by such self-reliance will you grow spiritually.

Even if the Truth be forgotten and lost by humans, it is always everywhere present and so can be regained. Truth, knowledge, wisdom, and love are eternal and unchanging.

Part III

Choices at the Crossroads

Humanity is faced with the option of continuing to follow organized religions or to turn instead to universal spiritual principles. It is this choice that could determine the fate of the world. The seven basic principles of spirituality that the Pleiadians have presented to Earth offer a philosophy that could save us from self-destruction.

CHAPTER ELEVEN

ORGANIZED RELIGION versus
UNIVERSAL SPIRITUAL PRINCIPLES

In the hope that humanity could be turned away from its self-destructive path, the Pleiadians contacted Billy Meier and taught him the universal principles of spirituality. They did this because of the compassion they felt for us. They see us trapped in false religious teachings that are creating suffering on a global scale.

We are guided by false dogmas instead of Truth. The Pleiadians say that if we turn to the seven universal spiritual principles they have presented—Oneness, Eternal Evolution of Spirit, Self-Responsibility, Love, Balance, Truth, and Equality—then we can create a world of peace, joy, happiness, and harmony.

For millennia we have tried to create a functional civilization upon this world, only to fail again and again. The Pleiadians told Billy that the primary reason we haven't been able to create a unified, peaceful world civilization is because we are so wedded to our irrational, dogmatic, authoritarian religions. Only when we turn aside from belief and instead turn to universal spiritual principles will we achieve world peace.

We need to learn how to discriminate between truth and falsehood, between belief and fact, between dogma and reality. We need to start applying the scientific process to our beliefs and to the ideas by which we live our lives. We need to examine and discard the fossilized ideas that no longer serve us.

Like concerned elder brothers, the Pleiadians are trying to help us grow up, to put aside our childishness and become sane and wise adults instead of irrational, immature adolescents. To this end, they have presented us with an alternative approach to life—a tried and true approach that has worked for them and for other civilizations throughout our galaxy.

The Bafath

The Pleiadians who contacted Billy were guided by love and empathy to do all that they could to help us. Unfortunately, other Pleiadians were not of such a benevolent character. All Pleiadians are descendants of Lyrians (ETs from the constellation of Lyra in our Milky Way galaxy) who had repeatedly colonized and then abandoned Earth over millions of years. They colonized the Pleiades and many other star systems in this galaxy. Thousands of years ago when these Lyrian/Pleiadians were living on Earth, they split into two groups—the malevolent, power-hungry Bafath, and the spiritually-minded ones we now call the Pleiadians. [Please see Appendix No. 1 for greater detail.]

The Bafath were a splinter group of Lyrians that broke away from the main body of their race because they still sought power and domination like their ancient Lyrian ancestors. The more evolved and loving Pleiadians living on Earth gained complete control of the planet and exiled the Bafath from planet Earth about three thousand years ago. The Bafath first went to a nearby star system but shortly afterwards they secretly returned and hid in a deserted city built long ago under the pyramids in Egypt. There, using their highly developed psychic powers to influence and dominate many world leaders, they plotted and schemed to take over the planet by encouraging blind faith and religious fanaticism, along with political chaos and tyranny.

Semjase told Billy that in the twentieth century the Bafath had 723 Earthhumans under their negative telepathic influence and that 27 of these contactees were world-famous leaders. Hitler was one leader that they psychically dominated and guided. Interestingly, in an article about Adolf Hitler's psyche in the May 1, 1995 issue of *The New Yorker* magazine, Ron Rosenbaum claims that in 1918 Hitler heard an inner voice telling him that his destiny was to lead Germany again to greatness. And no one has ever been able to adequately explain Hitler's extraordinary charisma and mesmeric power over the German populace. Perhaps his powers were derived telepathically from the Bafath.

Quite possibly the Shroud of Turin (a piece of cloth that purportedly was the burial shroud of Jmmanuel/Jesus Christ) was a Bafath creation. With their highly advanced technology, they could easily have fabricated such a thing in the fourteenth century (this is when carbon dating places the origin of the Shroud).

According to Semjase, the miracle of Fatima, which occurred from May 13 to October 13, 1917 at Fatima, Portugal, was a hoax perpetrated by the Bafath. The Bafath used one of their beamships (much like a Pleiadian beamship) to create the "miracle" of a shining sun. And they used their telepathic abilities to project images and thoughts into three Portuguese children, deceiving them into believing that Mother Mary was talking to them, and that Mary was giving the world a warning that it must turn to Catholicism or suffer global catastrophe!

The Bafath and the Baha'i Faith

And while the Pleiadians do not say anything about the Baha'i Faith, it is my personal suspicion that this world religion (which started in Persia in the middle of the last century) may well have been created by the Bafath in an attempt to create a religion that could eventually facilitate their attaining world domination. The goal of the Bafath was to encourage religious fanaticism and social unrest so that the world would become so chaotic that Earth humanity would welcome the Bafath as saviors and rescuers, and thus they would take over the planet as all-powerful rulers. [It is curious that the words *Bafath* and *Baha'i Faith* are almost perfect anagrams of each other.]

The Baha'i Faith was founded in 1844 in Iran by a Persian named Baha'u'llah (and by another Persian called The Bab, who was the herald for Baha'u'llah). They claimed that this new religion will be the law for the entire planet and that it will bring universal peace and harmony to the whole world because it is a divinely-created religion.

The Baha'i Faith is a religion out of the same mold as Christianity and Islam. It has three basic tenets, according to William Hatcher and J. Douglas Martin's book, *The Baha'i Faith—the Emerging Global Religion.* These three principles are oneness of God, oneness of mankind, and the fundamental unity of religion.

1. The first principle states that God exists and is a supernatural being who is omnipotent, omniscient, and is too great for a human to comprehend. This God is the ruler of the universe and mankind must obey Him absolutely.

2. The second principle states that humanity is one species and even though there are different races and ethnic groups, all are inherently equal.

3. The third principle states that God sends messengers to progressively reveal religion to humanity. These messengers, or prophets of God, reveal the truth in a gradual way so mankind can evolve little by little. No religion opposes another; rather, they are different steps in man's eternal education.

Hatcher and Martin say that the Baha'i Faith emphasizes equality between the sexes, unity between science and religion, independent investigation of truth (no ministry or priesthood), abandonment of prejudice and superstition, universal education, economic justice for all and the abolition of extremes of poverty and great wealth, having one auxiliary international language, and the spiritual foundation of society. The latter means that there would be a world government based on Baha'i principles. Thus the governing body of the Baha'i Faith would also be the ruling body for the secular world as well. The Baha'is have a very specific plan for taking over the world and governing it and creating a unified world.

Baha'is encourage interracial marriage, and they place great emphasis upon the importance of hospitality and treating everyone with love, kindness, and compassion. There is much about the Baha'i Faith that is truly commendable, and it is possible that in the near future, a sizable portion of humanity might very well turn to that religion to create a new world order. But it is with very mixed feelings that I say that. The Baha'i Faith totally denies any validity whatsoever to the principle of reincarnation and it is an extremely authoritarian religion that has a rule for just about everything. The book of rules that you must obey and that tells you how and what you may and may not do is interminable, reaching into every area of one's personal life

Instead of reincarnation, you are told that you must develop yourself while on Earth, else when you die and go to the Abha Kingdom—Heaven, that is—you arrive with deficient qualities and are thus prevented from growing spiritually within Heaven for eternity. To be insufficiently developed in character and thus be prevented from evolving spiritually is equivalent to being condemned to hell, according to Baha'i beliefs. So followers are under great pressure to follow the commandments and the rules and regulations, or else they risk eternal "stagnation" (certainly a kinder fate than the torments of eternal "damnation" that supposedly awaits fallen Catholics and those who stray from the Bible-based fundamentalist sects).

One of their most unusual—and dangerous—tenets is that the followers must absolutely and unquestionably obey their government, no matter how corrupt and evil it has become. They are to never revolt or try in any way to secretly undermine or subvert their government. Could this be a preparation for an eventual dictatorship ruling over humanity?

The God of the Baha'i Faith is very much like the God of the Old Testament. He is an angry, vengeful, unforgiving, fear-evoking God of power and might. Combine that with all the dos and don'ts of the religion that you have to obey, and it all can easily make a neurotic mess of one's mind. You become caught between what you are and what you "should" be—between what you want to do and what you are forbidden to do. The refusal to accept reincarnation and the extreme emphasis on a "God" figure are what make this a religion that if followed will, in my opinion, hinder the true spiritual development of humanity.

I suspect that the miracle of the Bab was also the doing of the Bafath. The Bab was a prophet in the mid-1800s who was a precursor to Baha'u'llah, and who prepared the way for the creation of the Baha'i Faith. The Islamic clergy at that time saw the Bab as a threat to their power and so they conspired to have him executed. They convinced the authorities that the Bab was corrupting the minds of the young and was perverting Islam, and the political authorities sentenced him to death by firing squad.

When arrested, the Bab was dictating a letter to his secretary. He told the arresting officer that he was willing to be killed but only after he finished dictating the letter. The commanding officer told him that he couldn't allow that and so the Bab was taken out and put before a squad of 750 soldiers with rifles. They tied him to a post and then fired away. When the smoke from the guns dispersed, the Bab had disappeared. But the commanding officer said that it wasn't a miracle, they had just accidentally shot the ropes off of him! Searching around for him, they found the Bab where they had originally arrested him, just as he was finishing dictating his letter. The commanding officer left town with his men, deciding that he wanted nothing to do with the matter. So another group of solders were sent and they arrested and executed the Bab.

For the Bafath, it would be a simple matter to position a beamship above where the Bab was to be executed and to surround the beamship with a light-bending force field that would render the craft invisible. Since the Pleiadians had such an advanced technology, the splinter group of the Bafath surely had the same technology which would enable them to cloak their beamship and to extend a force-field around the Bab's body, thus protecting him and creating a seemingly divine miracle in which only the ropes were shot off of him. People would then, quite naturally, assume that "God" had protected his divinely appointed messenger (until he allowed him to be killed, after the Bab had finished his last letter), and that we should obey whatever the Bab and his successor Baha'u'llah demanded of us.

In 1978 the Pleiadians removed all the Bafath from Earth and destroyed their underground city beneath the pyramids after the Bafath tried to openly assassinate Billy Meier. The Bafath regarded Billy as a great threat to their goal of world domination because he was revealing the truth about them to the world. They had tried to secretly kill him previously, but each time Billy escaped unharmed. Then, in desperation, the Bafath tried to openly attack him with one of their beamships. They attempted to bomb Billy's house—which would have killed his entire family. The Pleiadians, who were actively monitoring the situation, moved in very quickly with one of their cloaked beamships and positioned it right above Billy's house, thus shielding it from the weapon systems of the Bafath beamship. This egregious attack prompted the Pleiadians to capture all of the Bafath and to exile them to a far-distant star system.

This action was the "checkmate" move that finally defeated the Bafath. For millennia the Pleiadians and the Bafath have been playing a cosmic chess game on Earth. It started when the Lyrian warlord Jehovan created the first world religion and declared himself to be "God." The Pleiadians tried to rectify the damage done by their warlike ancestors by bringing Jmmanuel to Earth to disseminate the teaching of true spirituality. That effort was blocked by the Bafath's influencing of humanity to distort Jmmanuel's teaching and to create the Christian religion. Then, according to Billy's recent writings, the Pleiadians created the Islamic religion to counter the advance of Christianity. Like the way firefighters use fire to fight fire, the Pleiadians used one religion to neutralize the other. And Islam did stop the advance of Christianity and prevented it from taking over the whole world. Then, I believe, the Bafath created another religion—the Baha'i Faith—in hopes that through it they could eventually dominate the Earth. The Pleiadians countered that move by having Billy Meier incarnate and then using him as a spokesman for spreading their teachings of Truth. The Bafath attempted to eliminate the threat Billy posed to their plans by trying to assassinate him. That was all the justification the Pleiadians needed to capture the Bafath and exile them to another solar system.

With the removal of all the Bafath, perhaps that was the removal of the power behind the Baha'i Faith. Maybe now humanity will freely choose a philosophy of truth rather than continuing to submit to authoritarian religions. How wonderful it would be if humanity would just adopt the best tenets of the Baha'i Faith and discard the religion itself.

Channeling

There are more and more books now on the market that proclaim to be channeled messages from the Pleiadians. Billy said that the Pleiadians were very clear and emphatic in stating that channeled information was extremely suspect and that most such channelings were simply the product of people's subconscious imaginings. If you read such books with a keenly awake and discriminative mind, you can easily discern the true from the false.

Many people around the world claim to channel a being called Ashtar Sheran, who presents himself as the leader of the Pleiadians. Semjase told Billy Meier that Ashtar was a member of the Bafath who broke away from that group and was in hiding. Even with all their technology, they were unable to locate where Ashtar and his group of followers were living. They didn't know what planet or even what dimension they were abiding in. Communications from Ashtar are of questionable value because, according to Semjase, only some of what he says is true. The Pleiadians did not explain in detail just what parts of Ashtar's messages were true and what were false but they did say that Ashtar was far more benevolent than the Bafath.

There are also a number of people claiming to be con-tactees of the Pleiadians and who are acting as their spokes-persons. And they are getting rich in the process. A little careful and objective insight into the character of these "contactees" will enable you to assess who is real and who is a fraud.

The Pleiadian Federation

The Pleiadians live in a society that is a federation of many worlds and that consists of about 124 billion humans. They have universal peace and live harmoniously with each other. They have gone beyond war because they have turned to true spirituality to guide their lives. Their decisions are based on logic, love, and truth rather than on fear, greed, and egotistical desires. It is this turning to real spirituality, rather than to dogmatic and irrational earthly religions, that is the essential next step for Earth humanity.

Ptaah, the father of Semjase, told Billy that only on Earth do such cultish religions exist. Truth—That Which Is—Reality—this is what people on other planets throughout the galaxy have for their "religion." Ptaah specifically said that although Christianity and Islam are the worst enemies of the Truth, all of our religions are cultish, heretical, and are preventing us from evolving spiritually.

Ptaah said that the ETs are quite concerned that humanity will try to export Earth religions and consequently spread discord throughout the universe. The Pleiadians, along with a number of other extraterrestrial races, are trying to educate humanity out of its dependence upon these cultish religions so that we can become attuned to Creation and learn to live in peace and harmony. Otherwise, when we achieve space flight, we will probably try to export our religions and our barbarism throughout the galaxy.

Earth religions do have their good qualities and, because there are many eternal truths contained in the world religions, they have helped and continue to help many people be more loving and truthful and happy. It is the dogmas, the falsehoods, and the rigid and irrational thinking patterns fostered by religions that the Pleiadians say are detrimental for humanity's spiritual evolution. If we are to evolve to their level, we must put aside our false ideas and turn to Truth, to true spirituality.

A quantum leap forward in evolution is possible by facing the primal cause of the world's woes and correcting that cause. We do what we do because of our beliefs. And our beliefs are essentially dictated by our religions. Because our religions are out of alignment with reality, we have a world that is inharmonious and is full of suffering. So the primal cause of the innumerable problems in the world today is our cult-like religions. By awakening to that realization and turning to truth, to true spirituality, we can come into harmony with life; and then we can have a Pleiadian type of society, one where there is universal peace and happiness.

Wrong Thinking

That religions tend to foster wrong thinking patterns is eloquently shown in *Feeling Good*, a book by David D. Burns, M.D. Although the book does not in any way deal with religions, the pathological types of thinking he describes are very prevalent in the religiously minded person. Here are some examples, in my own words, of what he terms cognitive distortions of reality:

1. **All-or-nothing thinking and perfectionism.** Black-and-white categorizing such as "If I don't get married by the time I'm 30, I never will get married." or "If I just believe in Jesus, then everything in my life will be taken care of and I won't need to take responsibility for myself." This category includes impossible and unrealistic standards leading to self-condemnation and guilt. "I must be as perfect as Jesus or I won't be acceptable in God's eyes."

2. **Mental filter and the magnifying or minimizing of the importance of things.** Selectively focusing on one small aspect of something and then exaggerating your judgment all out of proportion and believing that that tiny detail determines the reality of the whole. For example, "Because I hate my high school English teacher, I am a terrible sinner and I am doomed to go to Hell."

3. **Emotional reasoning.** "Because I feel this so intensely, it must be true." Or, "Because I felt so much more elated when I prayed to God in a Catholic church than in a Protestant church, the God of the Catholics must be the real God."

4. **"Should" reasoning.** "The Bible says I should love everyone or I won't go to Heaven after I die." Or, "I should go to confession regularly or else I'll be barred from Paradise."

5. **Overgeneralizing, labeling, and mislabeling.** "My latest business deal failed. Therefore I'm a total failure in life—I was born to lose." Or, "Only Christians can go to Heaven and all others are worthless sinners who are doomed, because Jesus is the only true prophet of God."

6. **Jumping to conclusions, magical thinking, and fortune telling.** Arbitrarily deciding that something is true without scientifically and rationally determining beforehand whether your conclusion is valid or factually correct. Irrational beliefs in omens and signs and the immature response to such. Believing that you can know what the future will be because of some preacher's prophecy. "When a black cat walked across my path, I knew that I shouldn't move to that neighborhood." "I'm going to sell all my property and give everything to my church because my evangelist told me the world is going to end next week and we will all be going to Heaven via the Rapture."

7. **Personalization.** You see yourself as the center of the universe and the cause of all external events. "My house burned down because I stopped going to church."

All of these wrong ways of thinking, which are so prevalent in our present-day society, must be put aside and replaced with logical, rational, mature ways of thinking if we are to evolve into a sane and peaceful society. Again and again, the Pleiadians stressed that our destiny is in our own hands. If we want a better world, we can create it.

There is a charming Earth fable relating to the principle that we have the power in our own hands to determine the outcome of events:

Once upon a time there was a tribe of Indians who had the custom of choosing their chief by determining who was the wisest of their people to lead them. Whoever could defeat the chief by proving him to be wrong about something, and thereby showing him to not be all wise, could then become the new chief.

A brash young brave decided he wanted to challenge the chief and so he cleverly planned to trick the old wise man. He would capture a little bird and then confront the chief by saying, "What do I have in my hand—a dead bird or a live bird?" "Then," said the brave to himself, "if the chief says that the little sparrow is alive, I will crush it to death in my hand. And if he declares that I am holding a dead bird, I will release it from my hand, and as it flies away I will then become the new chief." So he captured a little sparrow and, clutching the bird so that only the tail feathers stuck out from between his fingers, he challenged the old chief to divine the status of the bird. The old man replied, "Well, son, that all depends on you."

The popular gospel song, "He's got the whole world in His hands," is in error—it is you who have the whole world in your own hands. And it is all of us collectively that make our world what it is. If we want the world to be different, it is our obligation as individuals to change our own lives. This and this alone will bring about a better world.

Pleiadian Spirituality

Most Earth people are accustomed to following a religion that has an all-powerful deity figure at its center. This facilitates a false sense of security, because one can believe that a father or mother figure is looking out for one's good. Pleiadian spirituality, on the other hand, is wide open— as open as the universe. It is based upon the truth that Creation is at the center of you. You must find a sense of security within your very own being by finding your inner connection with Creation.

Pleiadian spirituality is different in many ways from Earthly spirituality:

Instead of duality and multiplicity (God, Christ, Holy Spirit, multiple religions, etc.), there is the principle of ONENESS.

Instead of Heaven and Hell (or nirvana and samsara), there is the principle of ETERNAL EVOLUTION OF SPIRIT.

Instead of saviors, avatars, gurus, popes, and priests, there is the principle of SELF-RESPONSIBILITY.

Instead of the often false and fickle emotionalism of Earthlings, there is the principle of unconditional and abiding LOVE.

Instead of the chaos, fanaticism, and imbalance so characteristic of the individual and societies on Earth, there is the principle of true and real BALANCE.

Instead of dogmas and falsehoods, there is the principle of TRUTH.

And instead of the widespread discrimination, suppression, and repression of women and minorities, there is the principle of EQUALITY.

These seven basic principles provide the foundation for a philosophy of life that is conducive to real spiritual growth and harmonious transformation of both individuals and society as a whole.

If these principles encourage you to be more free-thinking, to take more self-responsibility, and to have more love and compassion for others, then this book will have served its purpose. By using these ideas for stimulation, inspiration, and encouragement, it is possible to think new thoughts, to broaden and open your mind, to learn flexibility of thinking, to expand your consciousness, and to be free.

The Pleiadian material is fascinating, enlightening, and exciting to learn about. But it is also very iconoclastic and challenging to many of our basic beliefs about life, death, God, etc. So when we are confronted with this cosmic viewpoint, we are compelled to do a lot of soul searching, reflection, introspection, and growing up. But isn't that exactly what we as a race need to do? We are destroying our planet, killing each other, and rapidly heading towards a hellish future. We need to stop and reflect upon our actions and beliefs and to turn away from the path of greed, lust for power, and ignorance that so characterize our behavior, leading us only to destruction and sorrow. Pleiadian spirituality offers humanity a real and viable alternative. Here is a way of truth that offers hope for a better future and that offers a rational and sane explanation of our past and present.

I believe that if we as a race will grow up, face reality, and evolve spiritually, we can have a planet where there is no starvation, violence, hatred, bigotry, irrationality, ignorance, or war. We can have a society that is peaceful and loving and where all are taken care of. For this to happen, though, we must put aside the false imaginings of our lives—subservience to an omnipotent and omniscient savior, rigid and irrational authoritarian religious dogma and creeds, and deluded and wishful yearnings for an anthropomorphic God who will absolve us from taking responsibility for our own growth. All this must be left behind. Instead we must face ourselves as we are, confronting reality as it is. We must arm ourselves with knowledge and clear thinking if we intend to create Heaven on Earth.

The message of Pleiadian spirituality is that we must learn to trust in Creation, to trust in life, to trust in ourselves, and strive to discover that ever-present blissful spirit of love and truth that is who we really are. Semjase said that even when traveling from star to star through the great emptiness of space, she felt the comfort of Spirit: *When you love the Truth, then you love what is perfect and wonderful, for the Truth embodies the spiritual kingdom itself and is also the way to the kingdom of wisdom. Then you are conscious of Creation here and now, in everything, everywhere. Even in the depths of space you are comforted by knowing that Creation is there with you.*

When we each see All-That-Is as ourself, then we will naturally treat all beings with love, kindness, and integrity. When we as a whole race do this, then there will be peace on Earth.

CHAPTER TWELVE

ANSWERING FREQUENTLY ASKED QUESTIONS

It is unfortunate that the Pleiadian material leaves a lot of unanswered questions. How wonderful it would be if we could simply talk face-to-face with the Pleiadians and have all our questions answered! Since that is probably not going to happen in the very near future, and rather than just leaving the reader hanging, I will do my best to present an educated guess at the answers to a few questions posed by some readers of this book.

1. Does everyone have to incarnate on Earth for 60 to 80 billion years before evolving beyond this plane of existence, or is there some way we can avoid such an interminable length of time in the physical world?

I believe that it is possible to greatly shorten the time needed to evolve beyond the physical plane. By diligent and intense spiritual growth through meditation and living a consciously spirit-attuned life, we can (relatively) quickly evolve to such a high state that we obviate the need for millions of Earth-bound lives. Having attained such a spiritual state of consciousness, we would probably reside mostly in the fine-matter realms and only occasionally incarnate into the physical realm, doing so primarily to teach others about spirituality. Since some of the Pleiadians are vastly more spiritually evolved than others, and these high beings function as the leaders of their race, there is no reason that some Earth beings couldn't also accelerate their personal evolution and become the spiritual leaders of our society.

2. Why the big gap in the Pleiadian chronology between 22 million years ago and then 228,000 years ago?

Semjase did not divulge much information about that missing period of time, as far as specific dates. She did say that in that 22-million-year period of time, the Lyrian civilization repeatedly self-destructed because of catastrophic world wars that set their race back millions of years. They would destroy their civilization through war and revert to a very primitive state and then take millions of years to build their culture back to its previous level, only to then again destroy themselves because of their barbaric wars. One of the reasons the Pleiadians are here on Earth is to try to guide us away from creating the same fate that befell the ancient Lyrians. Perhaps the reason we haven't yet had a global nuclear war is because of the Pleiadian influence.

3. Do we dissolve into nothingness when the universe goes into a sleep state for 311 trillion years? Do the fine-matter realms also disappear during the sleep times of the universe? And what happens when the next universe day state begins? Do we start all over or pick up where everything left off at the end of the last day state? Do we even exist as individuals during the next day state?

Because evolution is always upward, forward, and positively directed, I believe that we will continue to exist from universe day to universe day. (Each "day" being 311 trillion years!) And I think it probable that the universe picks up where it left off, just as we begin a new day when the sun comes up anew each morning. And the fine-matter realms probably continue on as is throughout the 311-trillion-year night state. So maybe all spirits continue to exist during the universe's 311-trillion-year "night," but they exist only in the fine-matter realm.

4. How can I escape from having to reincarnate on this planet?

Evolve spiritually to such a degree that you don't need material incarnations anymore. Help humanity to evolve into a star-traveling civilization and then emigrate to another star system.

5. Does God still love us? Is this universe a safe place to live?

Creation is all love and all light. And we are loved by Creation. The nature of the universe is neutral-benevolent. This neutral character of the universe is exemplified by our freedom of choice as to what we do in life and our freedom to create happiness or misery by our choices. The benevolent aspect of the universe can be experienced in meditation where one experiences the indescribable bliss of Creation. That we are capable of loving one another is also indicative of the inherently benevolent nature of life.

Because there is no death as we think of it—that is, there is no annihilation of the spirit at the time of the death of the physical body—the universe is a safe place to be in terms of our spirit. But our physical bodies are quite vulnerable and need to be protected. Hence, it is prudent to be cautious and well-prepared for all of life's challenges.

6. What part does meditation play in spiritual development?

Meditation is an essential component of spiritual development. The deeper one can go in meditation, the greater one's spiritual evolution, if one is emotionally balanced and mature. It is possible to be an advanced meditator and to experience great bliss and high states of consciousness and yet still be a cruel, unloving, duplicitous, manipulative, exploitative criminal! I have met "spiritual" teachers who are living proof of that. They have tremendous bliss and psychic powers, but don't know how to love. And they mercilessly exploit their followers. So, meditation is not all there is to spiritual growth. Truth must be balanced with love and humility.

7. *Before reading this book I felt safe and comfortable, believing that God and Jesus were looking after me. Now I feel alone and on my own and I feel insecure and frightened. What can I believe in anymore?*

Follow the light, not the lamp. The light of truth has shown through many historical spiritual leaders. If you are too attached to a particular "lamp"—Jesus or any other past leader—you will be unable to appreciate the light that might be shining through a contemporary teacher or book of truth. The bottom line is to follow your own heart, not anyone else. Find the truth wherever you can. Creation is love. Awaken to your eternal connection with Creation and from that realization you will experience true security. Remember that aloneness is just the incomplete experiencing of all-oneness. If you are bothered by feeling alone, learn to face it and fully be with it and learn the lessons aloneness can teach. Then your aloneness will become all-oneness and the feelings of fear and insecurity will change into feelings of love, bliss, and radiant happiness that are reflective of the Great-All-Oneness. Have faith in truth, in love, in yourself, and in Creation. Man-made religions are not worthy of your faith.

8. *Are my closest friends and relatives all part of a collective soul of seven spirits?*

Quite likely. We seem to incarnate in groups, learning and interacting together with the same spirits lifetime after lifetime. In one incarnation we will be a father to a kindred soul. Then, in the next lifetime we might be the husband or brother or sister to that spirit. Over many lifetimes, we perfect and polish the numerous facets of the jewel of love.

9. What happens when I die? And what is the fine-matter realm like?

When you die you are the same as before you died, at least in terms of your character and your level of wisdom and knowledge. You separate from your physical body at death and that body then decomposes back into the earth. Then, accompanied by your loved ones who have died before you, your spirit body ascends to the vibratory plane most in harmony with the level of spirituality that you have achieved through your incarnation on Earth. There you review and reflect upon all that transpired for you during your earthly life. And from that study you glean the spiritual lessons you had assigned to yourself to learn on Earth. In the fine-matter realms, you continue to learn and grow spiritually. Different realms are apparently light-filled and blissful, while others are dark and are inhabited by miserable people who refuse to awaken to the ever-present light and love of Creation. For more information, you can read *Autobiography of a Yogi,* by Paramahansa Yogananda, where he talks about the many different realms in the fine-matter plane. Also, the three books by Anthony Borgia *(Life in the World Unseen, More about Life in the World Unseen, and Here and Hereafter),* explain in great detail the heavenly realms according to a British viewpoint. The two books by Helen Greaves, *Testimony of Light* and *The Challenging Light,* give a complementary perspective of the after-life world. And there is an ever-increasing body of literature on near-death experiences which sheds light on the nature of the fine-matter realm.

10. *Why didn't the Pleiadians go into the future and thereby foresee the failure of their mission here and consequently take different actions to better disseminate their information to Earth society?*

The future is always in flux. What we do today changes what will happen tomorrow. So the Pleiadians couldn't possibly foresee that humanity would so vehemently reject Billy Meier's message of warning from them. They tried their best, just as did Billy.

11. *If the Pleiadians are so advanced and so powerful, why don't they take over the world and save us from ourselves? And why don't they show their beamships publicly and thereby change the narrow-minded viewpoint of most people into one that acknowledges extraterrestrials?*

Our lives are our responsibility. Evolutionary law demands that we grow and evolve by ourselves. The Pleiadians can't and won't do our evolving for us. They can suggest we do this or that, but they won't force us to behave rationally and intelligently. They want us to come to that realization by free choice rather than compulsion. If we insist upon destroying ourselves through atomic warfare or suicidal ecological abuse of our home planet, that is not their problem. Creational law dictates that free choice should be honored. If the Pleiadians exposed their beamships to the public in a massive way, it would force people to acknowledge their existence and perhaps revere or fear them as gods or demons. The growth step of acknowledging extraterrestrial life should be a voluntary step that each individual takes on their own rather than having it forced upon them.

There is some evidence to suggest that the Pleiadians would prevent us from totally destroying the planet. That sort of catastrophe has already happened once before in this solar system. The asteroid belt between Mars and Jupiter used to be a planet inhabited by the ancient ancestors of the Pleiadians. Through atomic warfare they inadvertently blew up the whole planet. One reason that the Pleiadians and other ET races are visiting Earth at this time is to prevent us from destroying planet Earth. We can wipe out our race, but we will not be allowed to kill the planet. Humanity is like a small child foolishly playing with matches in a wooden house. This situation has attracted the concerned attention of many galactic races.

12. How human are the Pleiadians? Are the Pleiadians from our dimension? If we went with them into their dimension 1/2 second different from ours, would we be less dense?

The Pleiadians are completely human. They could mingle with us and we would not be able to discern any difference between them and us. Actually, they claim that sometimes they do visit Earth societies and mingle with the populace without being recognized as aliens. They originated in this dimension and lived on Earth, but they now live in a slightly different dimension into which they were accidentally thrust many millennia ago when they were fleeing an Earthly civil war. They flew in their beamships to the Pleiades through hyperspace, and when they reemerged, they discovered that they had crossed into a different dimension. That dimension afforded them sanctuary and protection against the pursuing enemy forces, and so they elected to stay there.

The Pleiadians are much more evolved than we and so have less dense bodies. If we went with them to their homeworld, we would still be as dense as when we were on Earth. The density of their bodies is not determined by the dimension they live in, but rather by the evolutionary level of their spirit.

13. If this is all true and it happened in the mid-1970s, why haven't I heard of it before?

Around 1976, Billy Meier had some of his beamship photos published in many different magazines around the world. He was interviewed extensively and for a while he was very much in the news. Unfortunately, his message that Earth was on the wrong path and needed to change met with fierce opposition. The Christian and Islamic forces did all they could to discredit him and his pronouncement that Earth religions were anti-truth. He was defamed, ridiculed, lied about, and numerous assassination attempts were made on his life. The popular media dropped him from the news. Even when Wendelle Stevens published some books about Billy and the Pleiadian material in the 1980s, the world continued to ignore the information. The present-day political and religious establishments have much to lose if the truth about the Pleiadians becomes widely known. So even today, UFO news is generally ridiculed and suppressed, or at least downplayed by the mainstream media since it is controlled (or very strongly influenced) by the political and religious hierarchy.

14. Where do we go from here? Apocalypse?

Some things are determined. They will happen no matter what. Other things are not determined. We can change them and prevent them from happening. The old saying that "the best prophet is the false prophet" means that by hearing a prophetic warning and then taking the appropriate action, we prevent that ominous warning from coming true. The Pleiadians would love to be such false prophets by having us take the appropriate actions, such as curtailing our population explosion, becoming ecologically responsible, and creating a unified and peaceful world. If we don't, the planet will cull the human herd down to an appropriate level. Perhaps this has already begun to happen with the appearance of AIDS and the Ebola virus and other viruses that are immune to our antibiotics. Either we get with the program or else we will have an apocalyptic future.

By our choices we determine our fate and how the future unfolds. The Pleiadians told Billy Meier that around the year 2000 there would be major changes on Earth, accompanied by earthquakes, volcanic eruptions, and other natural disasters, as well as wars that would kill a large portion of humanity. They say that it is our thoughts and actions that help create such upheavals. If we would attune ourselves to spirit, to Creation, we would have a much more stable climate and peaceful planet.

Semjase told Billy that in a few centuries Earth humanity would eventually come around to accepting their message about spirituality, reality, and what life is really about. And in about 800 years from now, humanity will have consolidated around this new teaching and will have created a far more functional and truth-based society on this planet Earth.

15. Why did you write this book?

I originally started writing this book in order to clarify and organize the information in my own mind. Then the project took on a life of its own, leading me to a realization that it could be of real value to the world. I decided to publish it and share it with others when I realized that the Pleiadian outlook on life could help save humanity from its headlong rush to self-destruction. The Pleiadian material can free us from our childish delusions about God and religions; and it offers a sane, rational, and truly functional philosophy of life. But don't take my word for it. Don't make me an authority figure. Try applying this teaching in your own life and see if it stimulates your personal spiritual growth and enables you to eventually experience an increased sense of maturity, clarity, understanding, balance, centeredness, and happiness.

16. Has anyone ever investigated the question of whether Jesus survived crucifixion and then went to Kashmir to live? And didn't the U.S Air Force's Project Blue book report prove that UFOs aren't real?

Actually, there are books that substantiate the Pleiadian assertion that Jesus (Jmmanuel) did not die on the cross but survived and traveled to Kashmir where he married and lived a very long life. Holger Kersten's book, *Jesus Lived in India, His Unknown Life Before and After the Crucifixion* (1986), delves into that subject in great depth.

Project Blue Book was not an impartial scientific investigation of the UFO phenomenon but was instead an attempt by the U.S. government to discredit all inquiries into the subject. There is an abundance of UFO literature that thoroughly investigates the Air Force's and other governmental agencies' attempts to divert attention away from genuine UFO cases and to undermine all serious investigation of ETs and the UFO phenomenon.

It is important to find out the truth about UFOs for oneself, to objectively investigate the UFO phenomenon before making up one's mind on the subject. To illustrate this, I will tell you a story:

During Galileo's time (1564-1642), the most esteemed scientist was a man named Creminino. He was the head of a scientific institute in Italy and was regarded as the top scientist of that era. When Galileo looked through the newly invented telescope, he saw that there were mountains on the moon. He invited all his friends to observe this finding. Soon, everyone was talking about how the moon had mountains upon it. This was most distressing to Creminino, since he supported the Aristotelian belief that all heavenly bodies were perfectly spherical. Realizing that he had to do something to maintain his position as the top scientist, and all the while refusing Galileo's offer to look through the telescope to see for himself, Creminino issued an edict. This edict stated that even though you saw mountains on the moon when observing it through the telescope, in actuality, there was a layer of invisible ice surrounding the moon that made it perfectly spherical. Thus, the Aristotelian system of belief was still valid. (And Creminino therefore was still the top scientist!) When Galileo heard about the edict, he issued an edict of his own. He said, "As anyone who will look through the telescope can see, there are mountains on the moon. But I will accept Creminino's assertion that there is an invisible layer of ice covering the moon. However, surrounding Creminino's layer of ice is another layer of invisible mountains of ice! So there are mountains on the moon."

I urge everyone to "look through the telescope" and objectively investigate the UFO phenomenon. If you will do that, you will discover that there is a basis of reality to it.

17. How much of this material is just book knowledge, and how much of it is truths that you have verified in your own being, from your own personal experience? What have you gotten from studying the Pleiadian information?

Studying the Pleiadian information has expanded my mind and given me the most lucid and liberating viewpoint on life that I have ever experienced. A lifetime of spiritual seeking is corroborated by their teachings. I have experienced the truth that all is one, that learning need never cease, and that self-responsibility, love, balance, truth, and equality are essential aspects of a life dedicated to real evolvement of one's spirit.

18. Who are the Grays and what is their relationship with the Pleiadians?

I suspect that the Grays, the bug-eyed little aliens that have been abducting humans and conducting medical exams and experiments upon them and who have also been killing and mutilating cattle, are the creation of ancient Lyrians. Grays are a genetically-engineered worker species that live for about 450 years and do not have digestive tracts (some abductees say they digest "food" through the skin of their forearms) or reproductive systems (they are clones that supposedly grow on vines!). There are different forms of Grays but most seem to come from the star system Zeta Reticuli. (Some do apparently have human-like reproductive ability and have been reputedly cross-breeding with humans that they have abducted.) Their fetal-like appearance suggests that they were created by genetic experiments with humanoid tissue that somehow was arrested in an early fetal stage of development. Perhaps the ancient Lyrians created them as a form of worker/slave and then when the Lyrians destroyed their civilization, the Grays were left on their own. They could have originally been created on Earth when the Lyrians were residing here sometime during the last 22 million years and then abandoned on Zeta Reticuli during one of the innumerable Lyrian civil wars that destroyed their civilization time and time again. Perhaps they have come to Earth because they are originally from this planet? That could possibly explain why they knew the location of Earth.

According to Randolph Winters, the Grays may have no spirit or soul and are doing experiments on humans in an effort to become more human. It has been reported that they want to change their genetic makeup to create a digestive and reproductive system and to somehow develop a soul that will reincarnate like humans.

Unlike the Grays, the Pleiadians do not abduct people nor do they mutilate cattle. When the Grays started abducting and mutilating *humans* in the late 1940s, the Pleiadians took the Grays aside and said that that behavior was unacceptable. Many UFO researchers say that it was during the Eisenhower presidency that the Grays made a secret treaty with the American government allowing them to abduct a certain number of Americans as long as they returned them unharmed, and to mutilate (kill) cattle for their experiments. Respecting the free will of Earth people, the Pleiadians take no action against the Grays, since our government has sanctioned their actions against people and cattle in exchange for scientific data. Our stealth bomber is reportedly an outgrowth of Gray technology.

19. What is the best way to learn more about the Pleiadian material?

Randolph Winters' book, *The Pleiadian Mission*, is the best overall introduction to the Pleiadian information. The books published by Wendelle Stevens, and also Winters' 16-cassette-tape series, *UFO—The Pleiadian Contacts*, are the most in-depth coverage of this subject currently available.

20. What is karma?

Because the universe is an expression of Creational One-ness, all that you do eventually has to come back to you so as to fulfill the truth of oneness. This cause and effect relationship is the principle of karma. Relating lovingly towards all will therefore yield the best future for oneself.

Perhaps this principle of karma was demonstrated when the Pleiadians met the highly evolved race of beings in the Andromeda galaxy. That happened at exactly the same time that the Pleiadians caused Jmmanuel (Jesus Christ) to be incarnated on Earth to help humanity to evolve spiritually. Maybe Creation rewarded that effort of the Pleiadians to help mankind grow spiritually by guiding the Pleiadians to encounter the race of beings who became the spiritual guides for their own civilization.

21. Do you believe that Billy Meier is the return of Christ?

I don't have any problem with Billy being the reincarnation of Jmmanuel (Jesus Christ). I believe that there is a strong possibility that he is just that. Of course, it is also quite possible that he isn't. But of all those who claim to be the returned Jesus, Billy Meier seems to be the most logical candidate for truly being a reincarnation of Jmmanuel. I don't know if he is or isn't, and personally, it's of no importance to me.

The *Contact Notes* certainly imply that Billy is Jmmanuel. In one episode, an amphibian-humanoid race of aliens whose starship was disabled in our solar system came to Billy to ask for his help. After the Pleiadians aided them and repaired their starship, Billy asked Semjase why these aliens had contacted him. Semjase told him that they had a herd-type of mentality and they telepathically singled him out because he was the most highly evolved spirit on planet Earth. These ETs assumed that he was the leader of the planet because with their race, the most powerful person is the "leader of the herd." She further explained that the Pleiadians lived in bases on Earth that were completely shielded so these aliens couldn't perceive them, even telepathically. It is reasonable that an alien race in need of aid would assume that Billy would be the leader of Earth if he really is a spirit from the planet Lahson and is billions of years more evolved than any other human on Earth.

The *Contact Notes* state that when Asket took Billy back in time to meet Jmmanuel, he was told by Jmmanuel that in order to help Billy confirm the reality of that meeting, Jmmanuel would have an extraterrestrial artifact buried with his body when he died in Srinagar, Kashmir. This artifact was a present given to Jmmanuel by his biological father, the Pleiadian Gabriel. It was a piece of some kind of foil made by the Pleiadians (like a small piece of tin foil). Billy did travel to Srinagar and retrieved the artifact that Jmmanuel had shown him at their meeting in 33 A.D. Semjase told Billy that it was completely appropriate for Jmmanuel to leave such an artifact for his own self to dig up 2,000 years in the future, which certainly implies that she believed that Billy was the reincarnated spirit of Jmmanuel.

I have never met Billy but I have spent time with people who have lived around him. They don't believe he is Jmmanuel, but they do say that Billy Meier is a good man who has brought an extraordinarily valuable body of information to this world. Whoever he is, I am thankful for how he has enriched my life.

APPENDICES

APPENDIX NO. 1—A Pleiadian Chronology of Earth

The source material for this appendix was the original *Semjase Contact Notes* and Randolph Winters' *The Pleiadian Mission*.

22,000,000 B.C.—Lyrians settle on Earth for the first time. Subsequently, they use Earth as a penal colony for their worst criminals.

228,000 B.C.—War in Lyra and Vega destroys 60 per cent of their populations. Asael, a Lyran Ishwish, and 360,000 Lyrians flee to the Pleiades and settle there.

208,000 B.C.—Pleiadians settle Earth, Mars, and Milona for the first time.

178,000 B.C.—Milona destroyed (and becomes present-day asteroid belt between Mars and Jupiter). Mars orbit changes, Earth evacuated.

178,000-100,000 B.C.—Repeated ET colonizations, including the use of Earth again as a penal colony.

71,364 B.C.—Pleiadians build pyramids in Egypt.

52,000 B.C.—Civil war again wipes out Earth colony.

48,000 B.C.—The Pleiadian Ishwish Pelegon recolonizes Earth with 70,000 Pleiadians. Civil war rages back on the home planets in the Pleiades. Finally, in the year 47,734

B.C., the power-hungry scientists are defeated and the Pleiadians adopt a spiritual government that continues to live in peace and harmony to this day.

48,000-40,000 B.C.—Pleiadians achieve higher and higher spiritual levels and make alliances with many different races throughout the universe.

38,000 B.C.—The Ishwish Jesas murders the commanding officers who succeeded Pelagon and he rules Earth as a dictator for 20 years. He then flees to Beta Centaurus when war again breaks out.

31,000 B.C.—Atlantis and Mu founded by Beta Centaurian refugees.

13,000 B.C.—Power-hungry scientists try to take over Earth but are defeated and so they flee Earth to Beta Centaurus.

11,000 B.C.—Easter Island in the South Pacific and Tiahuanaco in South America settled by giant ETs. The Beta Centaurians return to Earth under the command of the Ishwish Arus, known as "the Barbarian" because of his extreme cruelty. His forces plunder and conquer the area now known as Florida. For 1500 years his forces carry on skirmishes with the forces of Mu and Atlantis.

9,498 B.C.—Mu destroyed by Atlantean war beamships using disintegrating rays that melt their cities to the flat nothingness which is now the Gobi desert. In retaliation, Mu scientists cause a large asteroid to alter orbit and to be hurled at Atlantis like an enormous bomb. It breaks into pieces when it enters Earth's atmosphere and hits the continent of Atlantis like a gigantic shotgun blast, completely sinking the continent.

9,000 B.C.—Jehovan (Jehovon or Jehoven), son of Arus, murders his father and takes over the Earth and instructs the original primitive Earthhumans that he is their "Creator." Earthhumans use the word "God" to refer to Jehovan, "God" being the word used synonymously for IHWH (Ishwish or Lord of Wisdom).

8,085 B.C.—Great Flood caused by Destroyer comet. (This changed our day, which used to be 40 hours long, to the present 24-hour day, and changed the rotation of the Earth so that the sun, which used to set in the east, now sets in the west.)

5,000 B.C.—Jehav, son of Jehovan, murders his father and takes over the Earth. Like his father, he also is a megalomaniac and falsely poses as the creator of all Earthhumans and rules over them with great cruelty. He too is called "God" by the Earthhumans.

1326 B.C.—Arrusem, son of Jehav, murders his father and takes over the Earth. But his two brothers, Ptaah and Salam, wrest control away from him and exile him, along with 72,000 of his loyal followers.

1306 B.C.—Arrusem and his followers, now called the Bafath, return in secret to Earth, hiding in an underground city built more than 70,000 years ago deep beneath the pyramids at Gizah. They try in vain for a few thousand years to take over Earth by lies, deceit, intrigues, and by fostering cult-like religions throughout Earth's societies. (By the year 1977 A.D., there are only 2,100 Bafath left on Earth.)

1033 B.C.—Jehova takes control of Bafath from Arrusem. He is called "the Cruel One" because of his barbarous nature.

103 B.C.—Kamagol I takes over the Bafath. He secretly dominates Earth's religions and causes them to become even more cultish, dogmatic, irrational, and blood-thirsty. Then his son Kamagol II overthrows his father and jails him for life. Kamagol II rules until his death in 1976 A.D. He is even more evil than his father. He guides humanity to commit numerous acts of mass murder during his reign.

63 B.C.—Brothers Ptaah and Salam who had been peacefully governing Earth, are succeeded by Salam's son, Plejos.

0 B.C.—Plejos orders that Jmmanuel (Jesus Christ) be born on Earth as a prophet of truth to the Earth races.

26 A.D.—Pleiadian expedition to the Andromeda galaxy discovers a world inhabited by a very highly developed race of people who are existing as semi-material/semi-spiritual beings. The Pleiadian federation of planets voluntarily decide to defer to this race for all guidance and governing of their peoples. The Pleiadian spiritual leaders form a high council to act as the mediators between the Andromedans and all the planets of the Pleiadian alliance.

33 A.D.—Plejos and all of the Pleiadians living on the Earth (except the Bafath) leave this planet and emigrate to the Pleiades. For the next 1600 years the Pleiadians monitor Earth with intermittent visits.

17th Century A.D.—Pleiadians return to Earth as observers and set up a secret base in the Swiss Alps.

1937 A.D. (February 3) —Billy Meier born.

1975 A.D. (January 28) to 1978 A.D.—Pleiadian contacts with Billy Meier.

1977 A.D.—Bafath taken off the Earth.

1977 A.D.—Wendelle Stevens begins investigating the Billy Meier case.

1979 A.D.—*UFO...Contact with the Pleiades, Vol.1* published (Elders).

1982 A.D.—*UFO Contact from the Pleiades, a Preliminary Investigation Report* published (Stevens).

1983 A.D.—*UFO...Contact with the Pleiades, Vol.2* published (Elders).

1987 A.D.—*Light Years* published (Kinder).

1988 A.D.—*Message from the Pleiades (Book One)* published (Stevens).

1989 A.D.—*UFO Contact from the Pleiades, a Supplementary Investigation Report* published (Stevens).

1990 A.D.—*Message from the Pleiades (Book Two)* published (Stevens).

1994 A.D.—*The Pleiadian Mission—A Time of Awareness* published (Winters).

APPENDIX NO. 2—The Seven Levels of Evolution

The source material for this appendix was the original Semjase *Contact Notes* and Randolph Winters' *The Pleiadian Mission.*

STEP ONE: Beginning Life

1. Primary development of the intellect and spirit.

This is the stage where a spirit first begins to have lives in the material plane. The life span is very short. Everyone looks alike. One's appearance is greatly influenced by all the experiences and wisdom developed over countless lifetimes, so as people evolve at different rates and go through different experiences, their faces begin to look different from one another. The human face changes slowly over the incarnations. If you could look at photos of yourself as you were in the last few lifetimes you would be able to recognize yourself, since the area around the eyes especially tends to remain the same over many lifetimes. The Pleiadians told Billy that Otto Muck, the author of *The Lost Continent of Atlantis,* was the reincarnation of Plato and that Otto's appearance was quite similar to Plato's. Plato was the ancient historian who first wrote extensively about Atlantis, and Muck therefore was naturally inclined to also delve into that subject. In that book there is a photo of Otto Muck and a photo of a bust of Plato, and the two portraits look practically identical. The Pleiadians also say that everyone begins to look alike at the end of the evolutionary cycle when all are returning to the Source of being after billions of years of living in the material plane.

2. Primary development of thinking of intellect and spirit. After 10 to 20 million years of lifetimes we begin to develop our thinking and to gain some wisdom. At this stage the being is simple-minded and can barely sustain itself in the material world. People in these early levels are often thought to be insane, but really they are just very young spirits who are undeveloped.

3. Primary development of reason. It takes twenty to thirty million years of incarnation in physical bodies along with rest periods in the fine-matter realms to get to this stage. Usually a spirit is in the fine-matter realm for 150 to 200 years between incarnations.

4. Primary development of intellect and spiritual force. The lifespan is longer now, due to the accumulated wisdom of many former lives.

5. Primary development of reasonable actions. Very primitive caveman-like stage. Ignorance of what life is all about. Rational thinking process just beginning.

6. Primary will-caused thinking and acting. Development of rational thinking and understanding. People starting to work together and to understand each other. Each being's appearance is unique, due to the different experiences and rate of growth in wisdom over the lifetimes.

7. Reason-conditioned leading of the life. Tribal life and development of languages. Reasoning and rational thinking now predominant in people's life.

STEP TWO: Reasoned Life

1. Primary development of reason. Material-oriented lives. First beginnings of questioning of life and seeking of answers.

2. Effective development of reason and its use. People are now rational thinking beings seeking life's answers, and they look quite different from one another. Vibrant emotional life arising.

3. Primary acknowledgment of reason and cognition of higher influence. Active seeking for the meaning of life and the understanding of the forces of nature.

4. Belief in higher influences but still lacking spiritual knowledge. Development of belief systems and idol worship. No spiritual wisdom or awareness of what is real spirituality.

5. Belief in higher forces; superstition; fear of evil and veneration of good; creation of religions. This is the stage where most of Earth humanity presently exists. The lack of real knowledge of Creation and Creational Truths and the fearful clinging to religion, superstition, and blind worshipping of "God" keeps much of humanity enslaved in ignorance. The average human spirit at this stage is about eighty to one hundred million years old.

6. Primary recognition of the true reality. Research; development of real knowing; first spiritual cognitions and their use: spiritual healing, telepathy, etc. This is the first stage of real spiritual awareness. It is the beginning of the search for answers, yet still without real understanding of spirit. The typical New Age follower and people who have great curiosity about life and want to learn more about spirituality are at this stage.

7. Primary development of knowledge and wisdom. The accumulated wisdom gleaned from millions of lifetimes is now creating intellectual awareness and the knowledge that there is more to life than just material existence.

STEP THREE: Intellectual Life

1. Higher development of the intellect. Higher technology. Second utilization of spiritual forces. Primary creation of living forms. People are now intelligent life forms that have developed scientific knowledge and greater awareness of spirit. Seeking understanding in how life really works.

2. Realization and exercise of knowledge, truth, and wisdom. Slow break-up of acceptances of beliefs. Development of reasoning destroys beliefs in myths, gods, and unthinking adherence to religion. This stage is the present position of highly educated Earth scientists.

3. First utilization of knowledge and wisdom. Development of high technology and advances in genetic engineering. Man is learning the secrets of the universe. This stage is the present position of some very advanced scientists.

4. Acknowledgment and utilization of nature's laws. Generation of hypertechnology. Second creation of living forms. Advances in science. Higher technological advances in genetics and cloning. Understanding of forces of nature.

5. Natural exercise of wisdom and knowledge in cognition of spiritual forces. More use of spirit in mastering life and its challenges.

6. Life in knowing about wisdom, truth, and logic. Beginning contact with higher life forms. True meaning of life is beginning to be understood.

7. Primary cognition of the true meaning of life. Real knowledge of the laws of Creation. Religions fading away. A few highly advanced scientists are at this level.

STEP FOUR: Harmonious Life

1. Clear knowledge about the reality as being truly real. Humanity has now developed harmonious living, clear thinking, and real knowledge about life and spirit.

2. Cognition of spiritual knowledge and spiritual wisdom. Beginning experiments with telepathy, telekinesis, time travel, and control over nature.

3. Utilization of the spiritual knowledge and spiritual wisdom. Working with the energies of all life forms. Solving life's problems with spiritual consciousness. Use of telepathy and other spiritual powers.

4. Cognition of the reality of Creation and its laws. Understanding of our connection to Creation and the real meaning of life.

5. Living from the Creational laws. Purification of the spirit and the intellect. Cognition of the true obligation and force of the spirit. Complete abandonment of dogmatic belief systems.

According to the Pleiadians, this stage is Billy Meier's present position. (The spirit of Billy Meier/Jmmanuel agreed to retrace many evolutionary stages when he came to Earth from the planet Lahson and incarnate as a human being of a lower evolutionary stage than the one he occupied on Lahson. The Pleiadians told him that when he finishes his mission on Earth as a spiritual prophet, they will take him off Earth to study with very highly advanced spiritual teachers so that he can quickly evolve back to the former evolutionary stage that he had on Lahson. Then he will be reunited with the group consciousness he left on planet Lahson.)

6. Directed and controlled utilization of spiritual forces. Living in higher consciousness. End of belief systems. Conscious obedience to Creational laws. Perceiving life from spiritual perspective.

7. Creation of first live creations. Higher technology developed. Man now exploring the universe. Ability to create life forms. Extinct species can be recreated by genetic engineers.

STEP FIVE: Wisdom Life

1. Creating and controlling of living forms. Life span now greatly extended through spiritual power and advanced technology. (The Pleiadians live a typical lifespan of 700 to 1200 years). Lives are now more spiritual than material. Acting as guides to less advanced civilizations.

2. Construction of androids (machine/organic forms). Greater concern for Creation and spiritual development.

3. Spiritual development of forces for control of material and organic forms of life. The force of our spirit has developed to the point that we can control the birth of other creatures. Controlling the forces of nature—gravity, electricity, and levitation. People starting to look and think more alike.

4. Will-conditioned mastering of life and all its forms. Becoming masters of all knowledge of the human form.

5. Position of recognitions. Reminiscences of earlier lives. Our spirit can control time and space, and we can recollect our previous lifetimes.

6. Kings of wisdom—called Ishwishes (IHWH). This is the level before the last highest power and knowledge. Mastery of human knowledge. Living in a material body but functioning mostly through one's spirit. This is the level of "god." In the past, the Earth was ruled by Pleiadians of this level who were called "gods." It was incorrectly believed by Earthhumans that these Kings of Wisdom had the power of life and death. There are no longer any Ishwishes on Earth but many people still retain the ancient concept of a god ruling over them. This disempowers them and postpones their taking control of their lives.

7. Cognition of spiritual peace and of the universal love and Creational harmony. Transition stage from material life to spiritual life in the fine-matter world. We are at peace with Creation and we live in complete understanding of life. We all look fairly alike since we have all arrived at the same level of evolvement and are now mostly spiritual rather than material beings. [The Pleiadians exist at levels #4, #5, #6, and #7 of Step Five. The average age of a Pleiadian's spirit is

400 to 500 million years old. So they are 300 to 400 million years more advanced than the average Earthhuman.]

STEP SIX: Spiritual Life

1. Acknowledgment and realization of spiritual peace, universal love, and Creational harmony. In this last stage of material life we live in harmony and we feel the constant love of Creation.

2. Living in pure spiritual forms. We are becoming pure spiritual forms that no longer need food or sleep. Our bodies become lighter and lighter as we transition out of the material realm.

3. Spiritual creations. Our bodies have become transparent since our existence is almost purely spiritual now. The death/reincarnation cycle has ended. We help educate and give spiritual guidance to other civilizations in the material plane.

4. Disembodiment of the spirit from organic matter. The material body is completely gone and we exist as purely spiritual forms. We are about 70 billion years old and live in constant awareness of love and understanding of life. We still have personalities and self-awareness. We act as guides of wisdom for younger races.

5. First spiritual existence. Spirits come together in a group consciousness of seven spirit-forms. We retain awareness of self while we participate in the development of human life. Millions of years pass by in this stage.

6. Final spiritual existence. This is the last stage of the collective consciousness of groups of seven spirits. Personal identity fades away as we reach the Petale Level, the highest level of consciousness. All collective consciousnesses come together as one in readiness for the transition to unification with Creation.

7. Unification with the Creation. The completion of the evolutionary process in which the independent life form transcends all separateness and reunites at last with the source of beingness. We now merge into oneness with the Whole. We become part of the total knowledge of Creation that gives guidance and love to all that exists. We now have completely understood the evolution of a universe.

STEP SEVEN: Creational Life

1. Twilight sleep over seven greattimes. We now enter into a period of sleep for seven greattimes, or an "eternity." During this sleep time the whole material universe ceases to exist. Time and space and all life disappear.

2. Awakening and beginning of creating in the Creation, as the Creation, during seven periods/greattimes. We awaken as Creation and begin to form a new universe. Awareness of oneself as a separate being is gone and instead we are one with Creation, helping it to begin a new evolutionary cycle with the formation of a new universe.

3. Creating of living forms. Creational energy has evolved to a higher level. Now it begins to create new life forms which will contribute to Creation's evolution through the wisdom gained from all the new experiences that they will be going through.

4. Creating of new spirit forms in improvement of the Creation. Creation is continually evolving by creating new spirit forms that grow and learn through material incarnations. Throughout the material cycle of a universe there are new life forms being created.

5. Creating of spiritual greatness in the Creation. Creation is growing in wisdom and knowledge, ever growing towards perfection.

6. Improvement of the Creation in the Creation. Creation evolves through seven cycles of material manifestation of a universe.

7. Last reaching of highest improvement in the seventh period/greattime. Creation achieves the highest evolutionary perfection and now transforms into an Ur Universe that is capable of creating other Creational universes. An Ur Universe can provide enough energy to create several Creational Universes at once. We are now, as an Ur Universe, pure spiritual energy. And the cycle of evolutionary advancement continues on and on, for eventually the Ur Universe becomes a Central Universe (whose function is not yet understood by the Pleiadians).

REFERENCES

Andrews, George C., *Extra-Terrestrial Friends and Foes*, 1993, Lilburn, GA, IllumiNet Press.

Borgia, Anthony, *Here and Hereafter,* 1993, Midway, UT, M.A.P. Inc.

Borgia, Anthony, *Life in the World Unseen*, 1993, Midway, UT, M.A.P. Inc.

Borgia, Anthony, *More About Life in the World Unseen*, 1993, Midway, UT, M.A.P. Inc.

Burns, Dr. David, *Feeling Good—The New Mood Therapy*, 1980, N.Y., N.Y., Penguin Books.

Deardorff, James W., *Celestial Teachings—The Emergence of the True Teachings of Jmmanuel (Jesus)*, 1991, Tigard, Oregon, Wild Flower Press.

Deikman, Arthur J., *The Wrong Way Home—Uncovering the Patterns of Cult Behavior in American Society,* 1990, Boston, Beacon Press.

Elders, Brit and Lee, *UFO...Contact with the Pleiades, Vol.1*, 1979, Munds Park, AZ, Genesis III Publishing.

Elders, Brit and Lee, *UFO...Contact with the Pleiades, Vol.2,* 1983, Munds Park, AZ, Genesis III Publishing.

Greaves, Helen, *The Challenging Light*, 1984, Sudbury, England, Neville Spearman Ltd.

Greaves, Helen, *Testimony of Light*, 1977, Sudbury, England, Neville Spearman Ltd.

Hassan, Steven, *Combating Cult Mind Control*, 1988, Rochester, Vermont, Park Street Press.

Hatcher, William S., & Martin, J. Douglas, *The Baha'i Faith—the Emerging Global Religion,* 1984, San Francisco, Harper & Row.

Kersten, Holger, *Jesus Lived in India, His Unknown Life Before and After the Crucifixion*, 1986, MA, Element.

Kinder, Gary, *Light Years*, 1987, New York, Atlantic Monthly Press.

Kramer, Joel & Alsted, Diana, *The Guru Papers—Masks of Authoritarian Power*, 1993, Berkeley, California, North Atlantic Books/Frog Ltd.

McWilliams, Peter, *Life 102—What To Do When Your Guru Sues You,* 1994, Los Angeles, Prelude Press.

Meier, Eduard Albert "Billy", *The Beamship Trilogy* (Videocassettes), 1987, Phoenix, Arizona, Genesis Publishing/Intercep.

Meier, Eduard Albert "Billy", *The Decalogue*, 1987, Alamogordo, N.M., American Office—FIGU Semjase Silver Star Center.

Meier, Eduard Albert "Billy", *Semjase Reports*, Hinterschmidruti, ZH Switzerland, Semjase Silver Star

Center. (Only the German language edition is available to the public. However, there is existent an English language transliteration that purportedly both Steven Spielberg and George Lucas possess. While very rare and difficult to find, copies of this English version are obtainable by the diligent seeker).

Meier, Eduard Albert "Billy" & Rashid, Isa, *The Talmud of Jmmanuel*, 1992, Tigard, Oregon, Wild Flower Press.

Muck, Otto, *The Secret of Atlantis*, (Alles Uber Atlantis), Translated by Fred Bradley, 1978, New York, Times Books.

Patrick, Ted, with Tom Dulack, *Let Our Children Go!*, 1976, New York, E. P. Dutton & Co., Inc.

Stevens, Wendelle C., *Message from the Pleiades (Book One)*, 1988, Tucson, Arizona, UFO Photo Archives/Genesis Publishing.

Stevens, Wendelle C., *Message from the Pleiades (Book Two)*, 1990, Tucson, Arizona, UFO Photo Archives/Genesis Publishing.

Stevens, Wendelle C., *UFO Contact from the Pleiades, a Preliminary Investigation Report*, 1982, Tucson, Arizona, UFO Photo Archives.

Stevens, Wendelle C., *UFO Contact from the Pleiades, a Supplementary Investigation Report*, 1989, Tucson, Arizona, UFO Photo Archives.

Thompson, Richard L., *Alien Identities*, 1993, San Diego, CA, Govrardhan Hill, Inc.

Winters, Randolph, *The Pleiadian Connection*, (videocassette), 1988, Atwood, California, The Pleiades Project. (Self-published).

Winters, Randolph, *The Pleiadian Data Book*, 1993, Atwood, California, The Pleiades Project. (Self-published).

Winters, Randolph, *The Pleiadian Mission—A Time of Awareness*, 1994, Atwood, California, The Pleiades Project. (Self-published).

Winters, Randolph, *UFO—The Pleiadian Contacts* (audiocassettes), Atwood, California, The Pleiades Project. (Self-published).

Yogananda, Paramahansa, *Autobiography of a Yogi,* 1990, Los Angeles, CA, Self-Realization Fellowship.

FOR FURTHER STUDY

The Pleiades Project (Offers books, audiotapes, and videocassettes by Randolph Winters regarding the Pleiadian material): P.O. Box 1270, Rancho Mirage, CA, 92270.

Genesis III Publications (Offers books, photo books and videocassettes of the Billy Meier/Pleiadian material): P.O. Box 25962, Munds Park, Arizona, 86017.

UFO Photo Archives (Offers English translations of the Semjase Contact Notes as well as investigative books about Billy and the Pleiadians): P.O. Box 17206, Tucson, Arizona, 85710.

FIGU/Semjase Silver Star Center (Offers slides of Pleiadian beamships, and books and pamphlets by Billy Meier): 8499 Hinterschmidruti, ZH, Switzerland.

ABOUT THE AUTHOR

Gene Andrade is a lifelong seeker of truth, and is currently working on a guidebook for personal spiritual growth. The following is an extract from his next book:

For many years I studied with a famous spiritual teacher who glorified yoga and meditation. When I realized that I was out of touch with my feelings, I then studied with a teacher who glorified emotions. Feeling bored after a few years, I then studied with a teacher who glorified the mind. Awakening to the reality that all are equal and that nobody should be followed, I finally went my own way. Now I follow my own heart and look within for the light to guide me on my path.

Along the way I have discovered a few helpful truths about spirituality:

Surrendered Service

Conflict is inevitable when selfish seeking is your main goal. Let selfless service be your main goal and all will be well.

Loving Acceptance

Love and accept yourself as you are—unconditionally. Then you will truly be able to love others.

To order items from
The Pleiades Project

Star Wisdom $15.00
  (Gene Andrade's presentation of the basics
  of Pleiadian spirituality)

The Pleiadian Mission $20.00
  (Randolph Winter's 264-page book which
  presents an overview of the Pleiadian
  material)

The Pleiadian Connection $39.95
  (One-hour videotape that includes more
  than 100 pictures of Pleiadian beamships)

UFO—The Pleiadian Contacts $139.95
  (Set of 16 audio tapes covering information
  from the 115 contacts between the Pleiadians
  and Billy Meier)

S & H $4.00 for first item, $1.00 for each
additional item. California residents, please add
8.25% sales tax. Send check or money order,
payable in U. S. funds, along with your name and
address to:

**The Pleiades Project
P. O. Box 1270
Rancho Mirage, CA 92270**